COLLINS
WORDPOWER

Superspeller
Graham King

HarperCollinsPublishers

HarperCollins*Publishers*
Westerhill Road, Bishopbriggs, Glasgow G4 0NB

www.**fire**and**water**.com

First published 2000

Reprint 10 9 8 7 6 5 4 3 2 1 0

Cartoons by Bill Tidy. Bill Tidy's website is at
www.broadband.co.uk/billtidy/

Appendix A 'Ways to Improve Your Spelling', Appendix B, 'Some Spelling
Rules', Appendix C, 'The Apostrophe' and Appendix D, 'American Spellings',
are taken with permission from the *Collins Gem Spelling Guide*, compiled by
Mary O'Neill. HarperCollins Publishers would also like to thank Bob Coole
for reading the text, and Fiona Mackenzie Moore for the entry on dyslexia.

ISBN 0 00 472371 6

Typeset by Davidson Pre-Press Graphics Ltd, Glasgow G3

Printed and bound in Great Britain by
Caledonian International Book Manufacturing Ltd, Glasgow G64

Contents

Graham King (1930-1999)

Graham King was born in Adelaide on October 16, 1930. He trained as a cartographer and draughtsman before joining Rupert Murdoch's burgeoning media empire in the 1960s, where he became one of Murdoch's leading marketing figures during the hard-fought Australian newspaper circulation wars of that decade. Graham King moved to London in 1969, where his marketing strategy transformed the *Sun* newspaper into the United Kingdom's bestselling tabloid; subsequently, after 1986, he successfully promoted the reconstruction of *The Sunday Times* as a large multi-section newspaper.

A poet, watercolourist, landscape gardener and book collector, Graham King also wrote a biography of Zola, *Garden of Zola* (1978) and several thrillers such as *Killtest* (1978). Other works include the novel *The Pandora Valley* (1973), a semi-autobiographical account of the hardships endured by the Australian unemployed and their families set in the 1930s.

In the early 1990s, inspired by the unreadability and impracticality of many of the guides to English usage in bookshops, Graham King developed the concept of a series of reference guides called The One-Minute Wordpower series: accessible, friendly guides designed to guide the reader through the maze of English usage. He later expanded and revised the texts to create an innovative series of English usage guides that would break new ground in their accessibility and usefulness. The new range of reference books became the Collins Wordpower series (see page 178), the first four titles being published in March 2000, the second four in May 2000. Graham King died in May 1999, shortly after completing the Collins Wordpower series.

Browse Articles

Introduction

Perhaps there are people who are always one hundred per cent sure of their spelling, but invariably it turns out that they are merely fooling themselves. For, as someone once said, there are three certainties in life: death, taxes and misspelling.

On the spur of the moment, how many of us can correctly write down words such as inoculate, fuchsia, abattoir, cappuccino, stupefy, bourgeoise, laryngitis? We're talking about common words here, words that crop up in conversation and in popular reading, not 'spelling bee specials' such as apocynthion, rhabdomyoma, shaganappy and eleemosynary.

Bad spelling isn't necessarily a sign of illiteracy or lack of intelligence; it's an indication that most of us are only part-way through the task of mastering the spelling and meaning of the vast lexicon of words in the English language. A faulty memory, poor word or letter recognition, but particularly basic human laziness, all contribute to standards of spelling ranging from the unreadable and inarticulate to irritating sloppiness and, in more erudite circles, the occasional but embarrassing lapse.

The difficulty with spelling begins with the way in which written English handles the sounds of the language. We use about forty different sounds to express ourselves, yet have only twenty-six letters in our alphabet with which to write them down. This means that many letter combinations have to double for different sounds; the four-letter combination *ough*, for example, is used to express no less than seven sounds, as in *rough*, *bough*, *dough*, *bought*, *through*, *thorough* and *hiccough*!

It is also a fact that whatever it is, the English language has a word for it (and if not will invent or adapt one in a flash), so it is no surprise that against the French language with about 100,000 words, Russian with 150,000 and German with some 190,000, the modern comprehensive English dictionary will place half a million different words at the user's disposal. As few of us manage to familiarise ourselves with more than 15-20,000 of these for everyday use, that leaves several hundred thousand words lying in wait to trip us up.

We also have to grapple with the problem that half the words we use are not 'English' at all. From the Vikings on, we have begged, borrowed and stolen words (and have had a good many thrust upon us), very few of which follow uniform rules of spelling. And these spelling rules, such as they are, all seem to bristle with inconvenient and unexplainable exceptions; the 'i' before 'e' except after 'c' rule is a typical example.

It really shouldn't surprise us, then, that the correct spelling of words will always remain a thorn in the side of English orthography and its users. Spelling manuals have been around for a long time, some grimly pedantic; some overburdened with so many rules as to render them unattractive and impractical; some so selective and incomplete as to be useless as references.

Collins Wordpower *Superspeller* attempts to overcome these objections but especially aims to provide a quick, authoritative reference to the most difficult-to-spell words, proper nouns and

WORDS BORROWED FROM VIKINGS.
'Berserk' is one.

names in the language. The compilation is the result of research in Britain, USA, Canada and Australia, whose populations account for about ninety percent of primary English usage. Also consulted were school examiners' reports, surveys conducted by newspapers and public education organisations over the past couple of decades, and the results of dozens of regional and national spelling bees in the US.

In most English-speaking countries spelling has turned out to be a compelling and highly competitive 'sport'. A surprising number of people take pride in their spelling skills, and few experiences are more socially embarrassing and ego-deflating than being caught out by a simple spelling mistake. Which brings us to the **Collins Wordpower Terminal Test of Spelling Skill** towards the end of this book. This brutal battery of quizzes is designed to test your spelling skill to the limit. You can do it, as they say, in the privacy of your own home, or you may be sufficiently emboldened to turn it into a stimulating, competitive tournament among your family, friends or colleagues.

English is a rich and bubbling brew, at the same time mutinous and disciplined, reinventing itself constantly, and capable of expressing the near inexpressible. That is probably why, today, it is held in the highest esteem as an instrument of global communication, of learning, of creative vision. It is already the first language of over 350 million people and the second language of a billion more. You can't beat it, so why not join it? Improving your spelling skills would make a good start.

Acknowledgements

The author gratefully acknowledges the following sources used in the compilation of Collins Wordpower *Superspeller*:

Collins English Dictionary Millennium Edition; The Compact Oxford English Dictionary; The New Shorter Oxford English Dictionary; the BBC English Dictionary; The Hutchinson Encyclopedia; The Encyclopaedia Britannica; Webster's New Twentieth Century Dictionary Unabridged; Funk & Wagnalls Standard College Dictionary; and by no means forgetting *A Dictionary of the English Language in which words are deduced from their originals and illustrated in their different significations by examples from the best writers by* Samuel Johnson, LL.D., Seventh Edition (1785).

The 2,000 Most Misspelled Words in the English language

Including anglicised foreign words and a few dozen real stinkers ...

abacus, abacuses

abate, abatable

abattoir

abbreviate

abdominal

aberration

abhorrent

abrogate

abscess, abscesses

absorption

abstemious

abyss, abysmal

accelerate, accelerator, acceleration

accessory

acclimatise

accolade

accommodate, accommodation
accompanist
accordion, accordionist
accrue, accruing, accrued
acetic (*acid*); ascetic (*austere*)
acetylene
achievable, achievement
aching, achingly
acidophilus
acknowledgment *or* acknowledgement
acolyte
acoustic, acoustical
acquaintance
acquiescence, acquiescent
acquire
acquittal, acquitted
acumen
acupuncture
address, addressee
adenoid, adenoidal
adieu [in Spanish, *adios*]
adjourn, adjournment
adjunct
admissible, admissibility
adolescence, adolescent
ad nauseum
adulatory, adulate
advantageous, advantageously, advantageousness
adventitious
adze

aegis

aeolian

aeon

aerial

aesthete, aesthetic, aestheticism [in the US the 'a' is dropped]

affidavit

aficionado

a fortiori

ageing *or* aging, ageless, ageism

agent provocateur

agglomeration

aggrandize *or* aggrandise; aggrandizement *or* aggrandisement

aggrieve

agribusiness

aide-de-camp

aide memoire

a la carte

alienate, alienation

alimentary

allege, alleging

alter ego

aluminium [aluminum in the US]

alumnus, alumnae [plural]; alumna [feminine]

amanuensis, amanuenses [plural]

ambidextrous, ambidexterity, ambidextrousness

amoeba

amortization *or* amortisation

amphibious

anachronism, anachronistic

anaemia, anaemic

anaesthetic, anaesthesia, anaesthetize *or* anaesthetise

analytical

anathema

ancillary

androgynous, androgyne

anemone

aneurism

aniline

animadvert, animadversion

ankh

Can bad spelling really be defended?

Recently, a newspaper columnist attempted to defend the bad spellers of the world, claiming that correct spelling had been turned into a modern moral virtue. Many famous writers couldn't be bothered to look up words in dictionaries, he wrote, and even Shakespeare spelt his name three ways. "We've become far too pedantic about spelling. Bad spelling may be careless, like having egg on your tie, but most of us regard qualities such as wit and originality as more important. It's extremely dangerous to put spelling in a straitjacket".

His argument drew a quick response from a female reader who was a secretary and thus needed spelling skills. "If he [the columnist] were to receive a 'wonderfully entertaining' letter from his bank containing numerous spelling mistakes or the same word spelt several different ways, would he not question whether such an institution was qualified to handle his financial affairs responsibly?"

anneal

annihilate, annihilation

annotate, annotator

annulment

anodyne

anoint, anointment

anomalous, anomaly

anomie

anonymous, anonymously, anonymity

antediluvian

antenna, antennae [plural]

antihistamine

antimacassar

antipodes, antipodean

aphrodisiac

apiary, apiarian, apiarist

apocalypse, apocalyptic

apogee

apophthegm

apoplectic, apoplexy

apostasy

apostrophe, apostrophize *or* apostrophise

apothecary, apothecaries [plural]

appal, appalled, appalling

apparel

apparently

appellant, appellate

appendicitis, appendicectomy *or* appendectomy

applique

apposite

approbate

appurtenance

aqueous, aqua vitae

arbitrage, arbitrageur

arbitrary, arbitrarily

arboretum

archetypal

archipelago, archipelagos *or* archipelagoes

areola [human tissue], aureola [halo]

armadillo, armadillos

armature

armoire

arpeggio

arraign, arraignment

arriviste

arrondissment

artefact *or* artifact

ascendancy

ascetic [*austere*]; acetic [*acid*]

asinine, asininely, asininity

asphyxiate, asphyxiation

asphalt

assassin, assassinate, assassination

assessable

assuage

asthma, asthmatic

astrakhan

atelier

attenuate, attenuation

aubergine

auxiliary
avocado
awesome, awesomely
awe-stricken, awe-struck

Model caught after spelling failed to come up to scratch

A 19-year old topless model who scratched insults on the paintwork of her brother-in-law's new Mazda car was caught when her younger sister recognised her poor spelling. Giving evidence at Redbridge magistrate's court in East London, the wife of the car's owner said she was sure that her sister had damaged the car. "I recognised the writing because of the bad spelling and the kind of words used," she told the court. Her sister, who had a grudge against her brother-in-law, was ordered to pay £500 compensation to remove the offending words, which included "gigolo", "coward", "thief" and "bastard". It was not recorded how she misspelled them.

---

baccalaureate
bacchanalia, bacchanal
bachelor, bachelorhood
bacillus, bacilli [plural]
baguette
bailiff
balalaika
balletomane
ballot, balloted, balloting
balsam, balsamic
balustrade, baluster
banisters *or* bannisters
banns
banquette
barbiturate, barbital
barcarole *or* barcarolle
baroque

barre

barrel, barrelled, barrelling

barrette

barroom

bas-relief

bassinet

bathyscaph *or* bathyscaphe *or* bathyscape

battalion

bayonet, bayoneting *or* bayonetting, bayoneted *or* bayonetted

beatific, beatify, beatitude

beaujolais

bechamel sauce

behemoth

beige

belles-lettres, belletrist

belligerent

bellwether

benefice, beneficence, beneficent

biannual [twice yearly], biennial [every two years]

bias, biased *or* biassed, biases *or* biasses

bijou

bilingual

bilious, biliousness

billet-doux, billets-doux [plural]

bimetallism

biopsy, biopsies

bisque

bituminous

bivouac, bivouacking

blancmange

bluer, bluest, blueing, blued

bogie [under-carriage]; bogey [golf]; bogie or bogy [ghostly]

bookkeeper

bonhomie

bon vivant

bougainvillea *or* bougainvilleae

bouillabaisse

bouillon

boules [the game]

bourgeois, bourgeosie

boutonniere

bouzouki

braggadocio

braille

bric-a-brac

briquette *or* briquet

broccoli

bronchopneumonia

bronco

brooch

brougham

brusque, brusquely, brusqueness

buccaneer, buccaneering

bucolic

budgerigar

bulrush

bulwark

bureaucracy, bureaucrat

Computer Spellcheckers

Computer spellcheckers should not be given the final word: it will always be extremely useful to have a basic knowledge of spelling. One journalist who writes technical articles for broadcasting journals is well aware of this. In the course of an article he was writing,

HE WROTE . . .	AND THE SPELLCHECKER CORRECTED
How to deal with a battery-driven Philips super heterodyne . .	How to deal with a battery-driven Phallus superheater . . .
how pleased older collectors are to get an Ericsson . . .	how pleased older collectors are to get an erection . . .
a good review of the book *Syntony and Spark*, a real encouragement to Hugh Aitken.	a good review of the book *Synonmy and Spark*, a real encouragement to hug airmen.

Although many first names and surnames are now incorporated into most spellcheckers, bizarre results are not uncommon. A letter addressed to Ms Hilary Abbot Wimbush managed to arrive at the intended destination although unfortunately addressed to Ms Hairy Abbot Wombat.

---

caballero
cabriolet
cachet
cacophony

caesarean *or* caesarian. [cesarian in the US]. Sometimes
  capitalised: Caesarean

caffeine

caique

caisson

calendar [of days, weeks, months]; calender [paper manufacture].
  See *colander*

calibre

callisthenics

calypso

camaraderie

camellia

camomile *or* chamomile

camouflage, camouflaging

cannibal, cannibalism, cannibalise *or* cannibalize

cantaloupe *or*

cappuccino

carat *or* karat

carburettor *or* carburetter [carburetor in the US]

carcass *or* carcase, carcasses

caress, caresses, caressing

carpeted, carpeting

carte blanche

caster [sugar]; castor [roller]

casualty

casuistry

cataclysm, cataclysmic

catalogue, cataloguing, catalogued

catarrh, catarrhal

catastrophe, catastrophic

catechism

cauliflower

cause celebre

caveat

cemetery

centenary, centenniel

cerebellum

cerebral, cerebrum, cerebral palsy

chaise longue, chaises longues [plural] *or* chaise longues

chamois

champignon

chandelier

changeable, changeability, changeling, changeover

chaparral

chaperone

charge d'affaires

charisma, charismatic

chauffeur

chauvism

chiaroscuro

chicanery

chiffonier

chihuahua

chinoiserie

chlorophyll

cholesterol

chromosome

chrysalis

chrysanthemum

cicada

cicatrix

cinnamon

cirrhosis

clairvoyant, clairvoyance

clandestine, clandestinely

clangour [loud noise; uproar]; clanger [mistake]

claque

clarinet, clarinettist

cliche

climacteric [critical period]; climactic [causing a climax]; climatic
  [weather]

clique, cliquy, cliquish

cloisonne

coalesce, coalescing

cockieleekie [Scottish soup] or cock-a-leekie

coconut or cocoanut

cocoon

codicil. codicillary

cognisance or cognizance

cognoscente, cognoscenti [plural]

colander [perforated pan] or cullender. *See calendar, calender*

coleslaw

colitis

collapsible

colloquial, colloquialism, colloquy, colloquium

colonnade

coloratura

colossal, collosus

colosseum or coliseum

combated, combating, combative

comediene

comeuppance

commemorate, commemoration, commemorative

commensurate

commiserate, commiseration

commissary, commissariat

commissionaire

committed, committal

commodore

communique

complaisance, complaisant

complement [complete amount]; compliment [remark]

concomitant

concours d'elegance

concupiscence, concupiscent

condominium

confrere

connoisseur, connoisseurship

connubial

consanguinity

conscientious

consensus

consomme

consummate

contemporaneous, contemporaneity

continuum

contractual, contractually

contretemps

coolie

coquetry, coquette, coquettish

cordon bleu

cornucopia

coronary

corpuscle, corpuscular

correlate, correlation

corrigendum

corroborate, corroboration

coup [takeover]; coupe [car]

coup de grace, coups de grace [plural]

coup d'etat, coups d'etat [plural]

couscous

couturier, couteriere [feminine]

creche

crepe de Chine

crepe suzette

cretonne

crochet [knitting]; crotchet [music]

croupier

cueing

cuisine

cul-de-sac

culottes

cuneiform

curriculum vitae, curricula vitae [plural]

cutaneous

cutthroat

cynosure

cyst, cystic fibrosis, cystitis [bladder];

cytotoxic, cytotoxin

czar

The importance of correct spelling, Victorian style

The following childhood rhyme, dating from the 1870s, reminds us of the importance placed by the Victorians on correct spelling.

"And so you do not like to spell,
Mary, my dear. Oh, very well:
'Tis dull and troublesome, you say,
And you had rather be at play.

"Then bring me all your books again;
Nay, Mary, why do you complain?
For as you do not choose to read,
You shall not have your books, indeed.

"So, as you wish to be a dunce,
Pray go and fetch me them at once;
For if you will not learn to spell,
'Tis vain to think of reading well.

"Do you not think you'll blush to own
When you become a woman grown,
Without one good excuse to plead,
That you have never learnt to read?"

"Oh, dear Mamma," said Mary then,
Do let me have my books again;
And my spelling book as well,
For I really wish to learn to spell."

dachshund

daguerreotype

dahlia

daiquiri

debonair *or* debonnaire

debut, debutante

deceased [dead, often the consequence of *disease*]

deciduous

decolletage

decor

defendant

defibrillation, defibrillator

deign

deleterious

delicatessen

deliquescence, deliquescent

delirium, delirium tremens

demagogue, demagoguery, demagogy

demesne

demonstrable

demurrer

demythologise *or* demythologize

denouement

deoderise *or* deoderize, deoderiser *or* deoderizer

dependence, dependent, dependency

Diaeresis or Dieresis

The mark " which is placed over the second of two adjacent vowels to indicate that it is to be pronounced separately rather than forming a diphthong with the first, as in naïve, though the mark is frequently dropped in this case (a word that could really do with a diaerisis is *cooperate*, which would clearly indicate the pronunciation as *ko-op-er-ayt* and not *koo-per-ayt*, but such a spelling is archaic). The mark can also be used to indicate that a special pronunciation is appropriate to a particular vowel. While diaereses for words are becoming rare, they still exist with some names: *Noel*, *Zoe*, *Chloe* and *Eloise* are well-known examples (the 'e' in Bronte is not strictly a diaeresis).

---

de rigeur

desert [dry sandy expanse]; deserts [as in "he got his just deserts"]
  See dessert

desiccate, desiccation, desiccated

dessert [sweet or pudding course of a meal] *See desert, deserts*

desuetude

detente

deter, deterring, deterrant

develop

dhow

diabetes. diabetic

dialysis, dialyser *or* dialyzer

diaphragm

diaeresis *or* dieresis, diaeretic *or* dieretic

diarrhoea

dichotomy, dichotomous

dilettante, dilettantish
dinghy, dinghies
diocesan, diocese
diphtheria
diphthong
dirndl
disagreeable
discernible
discombobulate
dismissible
dissimilar, dissimilarity
dissociate, dissociation

The Diary of Charlie Scott, eight and a half

Aprall 17, 1855: I started from bath wis the imprecherin that I was going to skoull at Paris but to my dismay my forbidding Muther gave me the overwelming neus that she had changed her mind, not withstanding wor an oful time I had had the hoping coof had not left me yeat. Sometimes I got quiet ouetraged wis mamma for not leting me ouet of dors and perteceurly wen she sead I was not to go and se Roben Houdin wich I had ben expecting to go to for about a weke . . .

Despite his poor spelling, Charles Prestwich Scott later became the youngest and most brilliant editor of the *Manchester Guardian* newspaper, now the *Guardian*. So bad spellers take heart – there is always hope!

dissolution

dissonance, dissonant

dissuade

divertissement

doctrinaire

doggerel

doily

domino, dominoes

To double or not to double – focussed or focused?

Here is a practical rule which, in the case of certain words, will help you to decide whether to double letters or not.

1. If the last syllable of the word is stressed and ends with a consonant, double the last letter:

forbid	*forbidding, forbidden*
commit	*committing, committed*
remit	*remitting, remittance*
inter	*interring, interred*
sublet	*subletting, etc*

2. If the last syllable is not stressed, do *not* double the last letter:

market	*marketing, marketed*
target	*targeting, targeted*
gallop	*galloping, galloped*
focus	*focusing, focused*
pivot	*pivoting, pivoted, etc*

double entendre

doyen, doyenne [feminine]

drachma

dumbbell

duodenum

dyeing [colouring]; dying [facing death]

dysentry

dyspepsia, dyspeptic

Dyslexia

The genetically inherited condition of Dyslexia is defined as 'difficulty with words', but in fact encompasses a broader group of symptoms at levels ranging from mild to severe. A dyslexic person will have problems with words on paper at some level, inevitably spelling, often reading and writing.

They will also have trouble with the sound structure of spoken words and with reproducing sounds in sequence, mixing up the syllables of long words – Mrs Malaprop may well have been dyslexic. This difficulty extends to the learning of other languages. The nerve connections for verbal and visual labelling are located in the language area of the left brain. In dyslexics these connections are usually poor.

People with dyslexia can be clumsy, due to imperfect spatial awareness, and often appear forgetful because their faulty short-term memory prevents them from keeping hold of an idea while working out what it means. Retracing your steps to find out why you went to the kitchen in the first place is a way of life for many dyslexics.

In spite of, or perhaps because of their difficulties, dyslexics often display outstanding talent and ingenuity. The day to day effort of building alternative strategies to tackle learning problems can produce highly creative individuals whose very strength lies in their lateral view of things. The PC term 'differently abled' could not be better applied than here.

The first published recognition of dyslexia in the UK was an article in the BMJ on 'congenital word blindness'. It was written by a school doctor, Dr Pringle-Morgan in 1896. Almost another hundred years passed before dyslexia was officially recognised. It was included in the Code of Practice on the Identification and Assessment of Special Educational Needs in 1994.

Current statistics reveal that up to 20% of schoolchildren may suffer some mild form of dyslexia with 4-6% presenting serious difficulties. Boys are more often affected than girls. The numbers of adults are harder to estimate as most have learned to be ashamed of their problem and become expert at hiding it. However studies reveal that 40-50% of the male prison population may be dyslexic.

Over the last few decades attitudes to dyslexics have shifted considerably and the shame of being labelled 'stupid' or 'lazy' is much less common. Supported education is continually increasing and improving, although it still tends to be tied to a word-centred way of thinking and has yet to properly embrace a lateral thinking, multi-sensory approach which would exploit more of the strengths of the dyslexics.

ecumenical

eczema

efflorescence, efflorescent

eleemosynary

elegiac

embarras, embarrassing, embarrassment

embouchure

embryo, embryos, embryology

emolument

empyrean, empyreal

enamel, enamelled, enamelling

enchilada

encumbrance *or* incumbrance

encyclopaedia *or* encyclopedia, encyclopaedic *or* encyclopedic

endeavour, endeavouring

enfant terrible

enforceable, enforcement

en passant

en masse

enrol *or* enroll [US]; enrolment *or* enrollment [US]

ensconce

ensuing

enthral, enthralling, enthralled

entree

entrepreneur, entrepreneurial

envelop [to wrap around]; envelope [for letters]

epiglottis

epitome

equivocal, equivocation

erogenous, erogenic

erroneous

escritoire

espadrille

estrangement

eucalyptus

eulogy, eulogise *or* eulogize

eunuch

euthanasia

evanescence, evanescent

exaggerate, exaggeration

excerpt

excrescence, excrescent

exculpate, exculpation

exegesis

exhilarate. exhilaration

exhorbitant

exhumation

expatiate, expatiation

expatriate

extirpate

extrasensory

extrovert

eyrie

Enquire or Inquire: Enquiry or Inquiry?

Although, by a fine margin, the *Collins English Dictionary* and the Oxford prefer INquire to ENquire, it still remains a free choice. ENquire is the Old French and Middle English form, while INquire is the Latinized version. Caxton (inquyred), Spenser (inquere), Bacon and Tennyson plumped for the IN prefix, while Chaucer (enquyrid), Shakespeare and Milton preferred the EN style. Some draw the find distinction between *enquire* (to ask a question) and *inquire* (to investigate). In the US, inquire is standard, as it always in *The Sunday Times* and several other newspapers.

---

facade
facetious, facetiousness
fascia
faeces, faecal [feces and fecal in the US]
fahrenheit
faience
fait accompli, faits accomplis [plural]
falafel
fallacy, fallacious
fallible, fallibility
faux pas
feasible, feasibility
fiasco, fiascos
filmmaker, filmmaking
finagle
fjord
flamboyant, flamboyance
fledgeling *or* fledgling
flibbertigibbet
fluorescence, fluorescent
focus, focused, focusing, focuses
foetid *or* fetid

Fishy Spelling – how 'fish' can be spelled 'ghoti'

The great playwright George Bernard Shaw ridiculed spelling and the fuss made about it, saying that while we used some 40 different sounds to express ourselves, the English language had only 26 letters in the alphabet with which to write them down. To prove how illogical this was he would demonstrate that *fish* could be spelt as *ghoti*:

gh	as in	cough	(f)
o	as in	women	(i)
ti	as in	nation	(sh)

---

foetus [fetus in the US]

forbade *or* forbad [past tense of forbid]

forbear, forbearance

forebode, foreboding, forebodingly

forego [to precede], foregone. *See forgo*

foreman

foresee, foreseeing, foreseeable

forewarn

forfeit, forfeited, forfeiting

forge, forged, forging

forgo [to go without or relinquish], forgone. *See forego*

formatted

fortieth

fortissimo

fortuitous, fortuity

forward [ahead]; foreward [preface]
frangipani
fricassee, fricaseeing, fricaseed
fuchsia
fugue
fulfil, fulfilling, fulfilled, fulfilment
fullness
fulsome
funereal
furore
fuselage
fusilier, fusillade

Gems from the GCSE

Here's a display of spelling gems from the English examination paper of a 16-year old that (believe it or not) earned a B grade: *cuicus, headake, bargin, libray, coushon, safaty, pationt, earlyst, simaler* (similar), *equaly, mearly* (merely), *appreachiate, familer, imeadiate, brouch, matiri* (materially), *cemitry, leasure, frerternali* (fraternally), *misalanios* (miscellaneous) . . . Does that make you feel like a genius?

But there's more! Asked to describe the landing of an aircraft, another student was awarded a D grade in GCSE English for this effort: *A preuer shape was apporching from the southern vally graerly they disitusis recililly design aeroplane circling above*. On a slightly higher plane, this earned a C grade: *The machine touched down with prissision in the rough mountquiness regane, with out even scraping its' serface*. Other candidates got C grades despite minor transgressions such as *polosy* (policy); *amitter* (amateur); *ensiatic* (enthusiastic); *morage* (mortgage); *headech* (headache) and *carm* (calm).

---

gaiety, gaily
gallimaufry
gallivant, gallivanting
gallop, galloping, galloped
galoshes
gargantuan
garnishee
garrulous
gaseous,
gasoline
gastroenteritis, gastroenterostomy

gauge

gazetteer

gazpacho

gelatinous, gelatin *or* gelatine

gelignite

gemmology, gemmological, gemmologist *or* gemology, gemological, gemologist

generalissimo

genius, geniuses [genii is not the plural except in the sense of 'spirit or demon']

geriatric, geriatrician

germane

gerrymander

gesundheit

geyser

ghetto, ghettos

ghoul, ghoulish, ghoulishness

gigolo

gladiolus, gladioli [plural]

glassful, glassfuls [plural]

glaucoma

glazier

glutinous [resembling glue]; glutenous [containing the protein gluten]

glycerine *or* glycerin

gnocchi

gnome, gnomic

gobbledegook

gonorrhea, gonorrheal

gouache

goulash

gourmet, gourmand, gourmandise *or* gormandize

grammar

grandeur

grandiloquence, grandiloquent

gratuitous, gratuity

grievance [causing resentment]; grievous [severe or painful]

grippe

groin [lower abdomen]; groyne [sea wall]

guacamole *or* guachamole

guarantee, guaranteeing, guarantor

guesstimate

gubernatorial

guerrilla [warfare]; gorilla [ape]

guillotine

gumption

guttural, gutturally

gymkhana

gymnasium, gymnast, gymnastics

gynaecology [gynecology in the US]

The illogicality of English spelling

Beware of *heard*, a dreadful word

That looks like *beard* but sounds like *bird*,

And *dead* – it's said like bed, not bead –

For goodness' sake don't call it '*deed*'!

Watch out for *meat* and *great* and *threat*

(They rhyme with *suite* and *straight* and *debt*).

habeas corpus
habitue
haematology *or* hematology [US]
haemoglobin *or* hemoglobin [US]
haemophilia *or* hemophilia [US]; haemophiliac *or* hemophiliac [US]
haemorrhage *or* hemorrhage [US]
haemorrhoids *or* hemorrhoids [US]
hairsbreadth

halcyon

hallelujah

handful, handfuls

hangar

hara-kiri

harangue, haranguing, harangued

harass, harassing, harassed, harassment

harebrained [not hairbrained!]

hashish

hausfrau

haute cuisine

hauteur

headdress

hegemony

heinous

herbaceous

heredity [noun]; hereditary [adjective]

hermaphrodite, hermaphroditic

herpes

heterogeneous, heterogeneity

heterosexual, heterosexuality

hiatus

hibachi

hiccup [hiccough is now outdated]

hierarchy, hierarchical

hieroglyphic

hijack, hijacking

hippopotamus, hippopotamuses *or* hippopotami [plural]

hirsute

histrionic

hoeing, hoed, hoes

holocaust

homage

hombre

homeopath, homeopathy *or* homoeopath, homoeopathy

homogeneous [composed of the same kind]; homogenous
    [of common descent]

homogenise *or* homogenize

homo sapiens

homunculus

honorarium, honorary, honorific

hors-d'oeuvre

hullabaloo *or* hullaballoo

humanitarianism

humerus [arm bone]; humerous [funny]

hummus *or* hoummos *or* houmous

hundredth

hyacinth

hydrangea

hymn, hymnal

hyperbole [exaggeration]; hyperbola [geometry]

hypnosis, hypnotise *or* hypnotize, hypnotist, hypnotism

hypochondria, hypochondriac

hypocrite, hypocrisy, hypocritical

hypotenuse

hypothesis, hypotheses [plural]

hyssop

hysterectomy

hysteria, hysterical, hysterics

IQ and Spelling Ability

A recent study of 114 pupils at Strode sixth-form college in Surrey found that although their IQs were above average, their scores in spelling tests were below the standard expected of the average 16-year old. Fewer than one in five could spell words such as *erroneous, accomodate, allegiance, eligible* and *villainy*. And one in three students misspelt the words *foreign* and *initials*.

---

ichthyosaurus *or* ichthyosaur

idiosyncrasy

idyll, idyllic, idyllically

imminent [pending]; immanent [inherent or permanent]; eminent [important]

immeasurable

immense, immensely

immobile, immobility

immovable *or* immoveable

immunodeficiency

impassable, impasse

impeccable

impecunious

imperturbable, inperturbability

impostor *or* imposter

impresario

impressionism

imprimatur

impromptu

incandescence, incandescent

inchoate

incisor
incognito
incommunicado
incumbent, incumbency
indefatigable, indefatigability
indefensible
independence, independent
indict, indictment

The ITA – Initial Teaching Alphabet

One of the most controversial methods of teaching spelling was introduced in the 1960s: the **Initial Teaching Alphabet**. Essentially but only approximately phonetic, it had a 45-letter alphabet which was described by one critic as "a cross between upside-down Serbo-Croat and Greek". Instruction in the 'nue speling' went something like this: "You can spell *fox* 'focks' or 'foks' but it doesn't matter because eventually we will tell you that it is really spelt 'fox'". While it had its stout defenders among educators, others pronounced the results of the ITA 'catastrophic'. Or, in ITA-ese, *kataestrofic*.

---

indigenous
indigent
indigestible
indispensable, indispensability
indivisible, indivisibility
inexhaustible
inexpressible

infinitesimal

inflammable

inflammation, inflammatory

inflatable

ingenious [inventive]; ingenuous [naive]

inherit, inheritance, inheritor

inimical

innocuous, innocuously

innuendo

inoculate, inoculation

inopportune

inquire *or* enquire

insistence

insolvent, insolvency

insommniac

insouciance, insouciant

instal *or* install, installing, installed, installation

instalment [installment in the US]

instil [instill in the US], instilling, instilled

insure [to guarantee or protect against loss]; ensure [to make
    certain]

insurrection

intercede

interment [burial]; internment [prison]

intermezzo

internecine

interrogate, interrogation, interrogator

interrupt, interruption

intransigence, intransigent

inveigh

inveigle, inveigling

ipecacuanha

irascible, irascibility

iridescence, iridescent

irreconcilable

irrelevance, irrelevant

irreparable

irresistible

irrevocable

irretrievable

isosceles

isotype

isthmus

itinerant, itinerary

Geometric Correspondence in The Times

From Mr Colin Dixon: Sir, Having just completed the marking of GCSE mathematics papers for a national examining group, I am fully convinced that the silly season is upon us once more. From the first 100 papers marked the following spellings of a well-known triangle were gleaned: isocilies, isosoles, isosceleses, isoseles, iscoseles, iscocelled, isoceles, isosclles, isoscles, isocoles, isoscoles, isocelesse, issocelles, isosales, isosalies, isosceles, issoles, isosillies, issocelles, isoscellies, iscolesces, iscosles, iscoelise, iscocelleses, iscosoleses, iscolilis, ososellese. On the assumption that words change by popular demand, then change is inevitable, but to which spelling? *Yours sincerely, Colin Dixon.*

From Mr Andrew Ashton: Sir, I read with interest the letter from Mr Colin Dixon concerning the spelling of isosceles. He counted 29 different spellings in marking 100 papers. It reminded me of an excellent mnemonic that would have been of use to his candidates. I learnt it in my school days at Newcastle Royal Grammar School and have used it ever since: *I saw our Sherpas climb Everest last Easter Sunday*. I wonder how many versions of the word 'parallel' Mr Dixon found? *Yours sincerely, Andrew Ashton*.

From Mrs Anne Mathews: Sir, Mathematics pupils have to be taught the meaning of the word 'isosceles' before they can use it. If a teacher explains that 'iso' comes from 'isos', Greek for 'equal', and 'sceles' from 'skelos', Greek for 'leg', surely the pupils will have a better chance of remembering both meaning and spelling. They will also realise that there is both interest and practicality in knowing a little Greek. *Yours sincerely, Anne Mathews.*

An Angry Sailor

Confusion over the spelling of isosceles can occasionally lead to startling suggestions, as the following correspondence, between a publisher and a retired naval officer, would indicate.

To the Editor, Collins Gem Mathematics Basic Facts

I am writing to express my disappointment that all attempts to assist my great-nephew with his homework using the Collins Gem Mathematics Basic Facts failed in abject frustration at your very serious omission of the word 'Icoceles'. Geometry lessons were instilled with a cane back in my day and one permanent injury and a great many thrashed behinds remind me that Icoceles triangles have two equal sides and two equal angles, and the Icoceles trapezium has two nonparallel equal sides. I may have served a long and honourable career on Her Majesty's warships since then and there may well be a new fangled computer replacement by now, but that the word should have dropped so far from mainstream use leaves me aghast. I refuse to accept less than perfection. This applied as much to my naval charges as it does to the books that I buy today. I suggest, therefore, that you administer, to your own wavering staff, some of the same disciplines that made me the feared and respected leader that I am – you will be glad that you did.

The letter drew forth this reply from the editor in question:
To –

Gem Basic Facts Mathematics

Thank you very much for your letter querying the omission of 'icoceles' triangle/trapezium from the above book. The correct spelling is in fact 'isosceles', and if you look at p.147 of your great-nephew's book you will see that both terms are defined there. Thank you also for your suggestion that we should punish our indolent staff with 'thrashed behinds'. I am a very great admirer of the novels of Patrick O'Brian, but I fear that we would face major problems with both trade unions and the law if we brought in the lash as a disciplinary measure.

---

jalapeno

jalopy

jalousie

jamb *or* jambe

jambalaya

jardiniere

jejune

jeopardy, jeopardise *or* jeopardize

jeremiad

jeweller, jewellery [jeweler, jewelry in the US]

jihad *or* jehad

jocose, jocular, jocund

jodhpurs

joie de vivre

jonquil

judgement *or* judgment, judgemental *or* judgmental

juggernaut

juicy, juiciness, juciest

jujitsu *or* jujutsu *or* jiujutsu *or* jiujitsu

jurisprudence

juvenescence, juvenescent

juvenilia, juvenility

juxtapose, juxtaposition

Near Misses: a 20-second spelltest

Even though you may look hard at some words, it's often difficult to tell whether the spelling is correct. Try these: half are spelt correctly, and half are deliberate mistakes. Answers over page.

1. anihilate	5. resuscitate	9. liquorice
2. lacquer	6. surveillance	10. resplendent
3. laryngitis	7. homopathy	11. umberella
4. afficionado	8. jewellry	12. chromosone

---

kaleidoscope

keenness

kerosene *or* kerosine

khaki

kibbutz, kibbutzim [plural]

kibitzer

kidnap, kidnapped, kidnapper, kidnapping [kidnaped, kidnaper, kidnaping in the US]

kitsch
kleptomania, kleptomaniac
kohlrabi [the cabbage]
kowtow

20-second Spelltest : Answers

1. annihilate	5. CORRECT	9. CORRECT
2. CORRECT	6. CORRECT	10. CORRECT
3. CORRECT	7. homoeopathy	11. umbrella
4. aficionado	8. jewellery	12. chromosome

label, labelled, labelling
laboratory
laborious
labyrinth, labyrinthine
lachrymose
lackadaisical, lackadaisically
lacquer, lacquering, lacquered
laissez faire
laity, laic, laical
lama [Buddhist priest]; llama [S American animal]
lamppost
landau, landaulet
langoustine
languor, languorous
lapis lazuli
largess *or* largesse
larrikin

laryngitis, larynx

lascivious, lasciviously, lasciviousness

lassitude

lasso, lassoeing, lassoed

laudable, laudatory

laundrette *or* launderette, laundromat

legerdemain

legionnaire, legionnaire's disease *or* legionnaires' disease

legitimatise *or* legitimatize, legitimise *or* legitimize

leitmotiv *or* leitmotif

leopard

leprechaun

lese-majesty *or* lese-majeste

leukaemia [leukemia in the US]

level, levelling, levelled

liaise, liaison

libelled, libelling (in US, libeled, libeling)

libido, libidinous

licence [a permit or authorisation] [license in the US]

license [to permit or allow], licensing, licencer *or* licensor

licentious, licentiousness

lieutenant

likeable *or* likable

likely, likeliest

likelihood *or* likeliness

lilliputian *or* Lilliputian

limousine

lineage [ancestry]; linage [number of lines]

lingua franca

liquefy, liquefaction

liquidambar

liquorice [licorice in the US]

lissom *or* lissome

litterateur

littoral

loath *or* loth [unwilling]; loathe [to feel hatred]; loathsome

locum tenens, locum tenentes [plural]

lodge, lodging, lodger

longevity

longueur

loquacious, loquacity, loquaciousness

loquat

lorgnette

louche

loupe *or* loup

louvre [louver in the US]; louvred

loveable *or* lovable

lumpenproletariat

luscious, lusciously, lusciosness

lustre [luster in the US]; lustreless; lustrous

luxuriant [abundant]; luxuriate [to take pleasure]; luxurious
        [characterised by luxury]

lymph, lymphoma, lymphatic

lynx

From bad to worse!

A large sample of schoolchildren were given a spelling test in 1984, and repeated in 1989, and it was repeated in 1989. During the intervening five years, misspelling increased noticeably.

	1984	1989
bargain	14%	25%
library	14%	21%
merely	26%	39%
politician	33%	41%
exaggerate	43%	56%
committee	57%	75%
leisure	22%	33%
sufficient	29%	38%
appreciate	24%	30%
permanent	45%	51%

macabre, macabrely

macadam, macadamise *or* macadamize

macaroni

machete

mackintosh *or* macintosh

macrame

maelstrom

maestro

maharajah *or* maharaja; maharani [the wife of a maharajah]

maharishi

mahjong *or* mah-jongg

mahogany

maillot

maisonette

maitre d'hotel

majolica

mal de mer

manacle

manageable, management

manikin *or* mannikin

mannequin

manoeuvre, manoeuvred, manoeuveable [maneuver etc in the US]

manque

maraschino

mariage de convenance

marijuana *or* marihuana

marquee

marriageable

marvelled, marvellous

masochism, masochistic

masquerade

massacre, massacred

masseur, masseuse

matriarch, matriarchal

mattress

mayonnaise

meagre [meager in the US]; meagrely, meagreness

meanness

medieval *or* mediaeval, medievalism *or* mediaevalism

mediocre, mediocrity

megalomania, megalomaniac

mellifluous, mellifluence, mellifluent

menage, menage a trois

menagerie

menstruation [female period]; mensuration [geometry]

meretricious

meringue

metamorphosis, metamorphosese [plural]
meteorology, meteorological, meteorologist

Murderer caught out by 'e' for error

One of the most bizarre cases of a murderer caught by spelling errors was that of Bruno Hauptmann, who in the 1930s was convicted of kidnapping and killing the 20-month old baby of American aviation pioneer Colonel Charles Lindbergh. Hauptmann collected $50,000 but was caught and convicted on the evidence of his ransom note. Hauptmann had a rare dyslexic disability which was adding extra *'e's'* to the ends of words. In his ransom note he spelt *Decatur Avenue* as *Decature*; and in his clemency appeal he spelt *half* as *halfe* and *own* as *owne*. In 1936 this was good enough to send him to the electric chair.

---

mezzanine
mien
migraine
mileage *or* milage
milieu
millennium, millennial
millipede
mimic, mimicking, mimicked, mimicry
minuscule
misanthrope, misanthropy, misanthropic
miscegenation
mischievous, mischievously
misfeasance

misogyny, misogynist, misogynous
misshapen
misspell, misspelled *or* misspelt, misspelling
mistakable or mistakeable
mnemonic
moccasin
modelling, modelled, modeller [modeling, modeled etc in the US]
modus operandi
moiety
moire
monastery, monasterial, monastic
monocoque
moratorium
mortice *or* mortise
mousse
moustache [mustache in the US]
mozzarella
mucilage
murmuring, murmured, murmurer
muu-muu
myalgic encephalomyelitis
myrrh
myxomatosis

The ligature untied

Caesar, manoeuvre, aesthetic, oenology, mediaeval, encyclopaedia and archaeology are words that once contained a ligature, either a joined ae (   ) or a joined oe (   ). The trend today is to separate them – very few keyboards accommodate ligatures, anyway – and to further simplify the words (notably in the US) by squeezing out one of the letters, resulting in esthetic, medieval, maneuver and so on.

---

nadir

naiad

naive *or* naif, naivety, naivete *or* naivete

naphtha

narcissus, narcissi *or* narcissuses [plural]; narcissism *or* narcism, narcissistic

nascent, nascence

nasturtium

nauseous, nauseousness, nauseate, nauseating

necessary, necessity, necessitate,

neophyte

nephritis

neuralgia, neuralgic

neurasthenia

newsstand

nickelodeon

niece

nighttime

noblesse oblige

noisette

noisome

nomenclature

nonagenarian

non sequitur

nougat

nous

nouveau riche

nuptial

nymph, nymphet, nymphomania

'PT' WORDS – SILENT LETTER

Ptantalizing Ptongue Ptwisters

The English language abounds with words containing 'silent letters' (doubt, psalm, knot, sword, solemn, etc) but perhaps none so strange as the 'pt' words in which the 'p' is silent. Here are a few of them:

> *ptarmigan* – a mostly white, grouse-like bird
> *pterodactyl* – extinct featherless flying reptile
> *pteropod* – marine mollusc
> *ptilosis* – a disorder of the eyelashes
> *ptomaine poisoning* – from eating putrefied food
> *Ptolemy* – the Greek astronomer and mathematician

---

oasis, oases [plural]

obbligato *or* obligato, obligatos *or* obligati [plural]

obdurate, obduracy

obeisance, obeisant

obfuscate, obfuscation

oblique, obliquely

obloquy, obloquies

obnoxious, obnoxiousness

obsequious, obsequiously, obsequiousness, obsequies

obsolescence, obsolescent

obstetrics, obstetrician

obstreperous

occur, occurring, occurred, occurrence

octogenarian

octopus, octopuses [plural]

octoroon *or* octaroon

odyssey *or* Odyssey, odyssean *or* Odyssean

oesophagus [esophagus in the US]

oestrogen [estrogen in the US]

oeuvre

offence, offensive

ombudsman, ombudswoman

omniscience, omniscient

omnivorous

onerous, onerously

onomatopoeia

onyx

opaque, opaquely, opacity

openness

ophthalmia, ophthalmic, ophthalmologist

opportunity, opportunistically, opportunely

opprobrium

optometrist, optometry

orang-utan *or* orangutan

ordinance [regulation]; ordnance [military supplies]

organdie [organdy in the US]

orientate, orientation, orienteering

ormolu

orthopaedics, orthopaedist [orthopedics, orthopedist in the US]

oscillate, oscillating, oscillation, oscillatory, oscilloscope

osmosis

osteopathy

otiose, otiosity

outmanoeuvre [outmaneuver in the US]

outre

outspokenness

overall

overrate; overreach; override; overrule; overrun

oxidise *or* oxidize, oxidisation *or* oxidization

oxyacetylene

ozonosphere

Perplexing Plurals

The plurals of some words can play havoc with spelling. You can have one *date* but several or many *dates*, but one *datum* or many *data*. Blame it on the Latin origins of much of our language. Thus we have *alumnus/alumni or alumnae, bacillus/bacilli, locus/loci, errata/erratum*, and *stigma/stigmata*.

But, confusingly, we also have *virus/viruses, circus/circuses, prospectus/prospectuses* and *minus/minuses*. Not to mention some plurals that happily accept two versions, such as *agenda/agendum/agendas* and *formula/formulae/formulas*. Rules about these are rather liberal; you just have to learn and remember these wayward plurals.

---

paean

pachouli *or* patchouli

paedophile [pedophile in the US]

page, paging, pagination

paleontology

palate, palatable

palette

palimpsest

palliasse [often paillaise in the US]

pamphleteer, pamphleteering

panacea

pancreas, pancreatic

pandemonium

paparazzo, paparazzi [plural]

papier-mache

papyrus, papyruses *or* papyri [plural]

paradigm

paradisiacal *or* paradisaical

paraffin

parallel, paralleled, parallelogram, parallax

paralyse [paralyze in the US], paralysis, paralytic

paranoia, paranoiac *or* paranoic, paranoid

paraphernalia

parenthesis, parentheses [plural], parenthesise *or* parenthesize,
   parenthetical

pari-mutuel

paroxysm

parquet, parquetry

parthenogenesis, parthenogenetic

pas de deux

passable

passe

pasteurise *or* pasteurize, pasteurisation *or* pasteurization

pastiche

pastille

pastime

pate de foie gras

pavilion

peccadillo, peccadilloes

pedal, pedalling, pedalled, pedaller

pedlar [peddler or pedler in the US]

pejorative, pejoratively

pelargonium

pencil, pencilling, pencilled

penicillin

peninsula [but Peninsular War and P&O (Peninsular and Orient Steamship Co)]

penitentiary

penniless

perceive, perceiving, perceived, perceivable

peremptory, peremptorily

perennial

periphery

periphrasis

perorate, peroration

perquisite

personnel

perspicacious, perspicacity, perspecuity

petanque

petit bourgeois

petit four, petits fours [plural]

petits pois

phaeton

phantasmagoria

pharmacopoeia [often pharmacopeia in the US], pharmaceutical

phenomenon, phenomena [plural]

phlebitis

phlegm, phlegmatic

phlox

phoenix [phenix in the US]

phosphorescence, phosphorescent

phosphorus [element]; phosphorous [containing phosphorus]

photosynthesise *or* photosynthesize

phrasal

phrenitis

phylloxera

physique

pibroch

picketing, picketed

picnic, picnicking, picnicked, picnicker

piece de resistance

pied-a-terre, pieds-a-terre [plural]

pieta

pilau or pilaf *or* pilaff [flavoured rice]

pineapple

piranha *or* pirana

pituitary

pity, pitied, pitiful, pitiable, pitiless, pitiful

placebo

plagiarise *or* plagiarize

plankton

playwright

plebeian

plebiscite

pneumatic

pneumonia

poignant, poignancy, poignantly

poinsettia

poliomyelitis

politicking

polyp

polythene, polyurethane, polystyrene

pomegranate

pompon or pompom

poof *or* poove [effeminate]; pouf *or* pouffe [cushion]

porphyry, porphoritic

poseur

posthumous

potato, potatoes

You say <u>potato</u>, I say <u>potatoe</u>

Just before the 1994 Super Bowl, former US Vice-President Dan Quayle appeared in a 60-second, $1 million TV commercial for potato crisps, for which he was paid a fee of $50,000 (later donated to charity). The reason for his appearance was his famous misspelling of *potato*. During a well-publicised visit to a New York school, while still Vice-President, Quayle instructed a 12-year old student to spell *potato* with an 'e': P-O-T-A-T-O-E.

The spelling gaffe resulted in a storm of mockery and Dan Quayle became a national laughing stock. Super Bowl XXVIII was between the Dallas Cowboys and the Buffalo Bills. Or as the V-P would have it, the Buffaloe Bills.

practice [noun]; practise [verb]; practised *or in the US* practiced
        [adjective]

preciosity

predecessor

predilection

prefer, preferring, preferred, preference

premier [head of state]; premiere [first performance]

presbytery

prescience, prescient, presciently

presentient, presentiment

prestidigitation, prestidigitator

preventive or *sometimes* preventative

The prevalence of <u>preventative</u>

Why use *preventative* when the shorter *preventive* means
exactly the same? In a letter to *The Times* a reader admonished
users of the former with this little rhyme:

Who coined the word preventative?
Was there an incentative?
For someone so inventative?
And could we hear of villains held
In custody detentative?

---

prima facie

primordial

principal [the chief]; principle [code of conduct]

privilege

profit, profiting, profited, profiteer

progesterone

proletariat, proletarian

promiscuous, promiscuity

promissory note

pronounce, pronounceable, pronouncement, pronunciation

propeller, propelling, propelled

prophecy [the forecast]; prophesy [to forecast]

prophylactic, prophylaxis

proprietary [ownership]; propriety [appropriate, conforming]

pros and cons

prosciutto

proselyte, proselytise *or* proselytize

prosthesis, prosthetic

protege, protegee [feminine]

protuberance, protuberant

psalm, psalmist

pseudonym, pseudonymous

psittacosis

psoriasis

psychedelic, psychedelia

psychology, psychoanalysis, psychiatry, psychotherapy, psychotic,
  psychosomatic

ptarmigan

pterodactyl

ptomaine poisoning

pubescence, pubescent

puerile

puerperal fever

puisne
puissance, puissant
pulchritude
punctilious, punctiliousness
puree, pureeing, pureed
puritanical
purlieu
pursuivant
pusillanimous, pusillanimity, pusillanimously
putsch
pygmy *or* pigmy [*or* as proper nouns, Pygmy *or* Pigmy]
pyjamas [pajamas in the US]
pyorrhoea [pyorrhea in the US]
pyrrhic

Pitfalls of word recognition

Just as it's not uncommon to mistake a person for someone else, we can all at times fail to recognise words. Here is a small collection of malapropian misspellings contributed by the pubic:

His record high jump was sheer poultry in motion
It is true that no man is in ireland
She promptly flew into a high dungeon
Unfortunately, his father died interstate
I wouldn't touch it with a ten-foot Pole
After the storm the beach was covered with jellyfish testicles
Tess was a strange child, and old beyond her ears . . .

quadruped

quadruplets

quagmire

quango, quangos [plural]

quarrel, quarelling, quarelled [quareling etc in the US], quarelsome

quatrefoil

quay, quayside

questionnaire

queue, queueing, queued

quiescence, quiescent

quieten, quietude, quietus

qui vive

quoin *or* coign *or* coigne

quoits

quotient

Ritn English

The organisation most critical of the archaic, complex and illogical spelling of English is the **Simplifyd Speling Society** (for that is how they spell it) which has issued a *Handbook to Cut Speling* listing simplified versions of 21,000 words. By using 'cut speling' the Society claims that:

* ritn english wud be shortnd by sum 10%, ofring signifcnt ecnomic benfits.

* english wud be esy to reed withut traning and can soon be red as fast as traditnl speling

* harmnizing variatns –such as head/bed/said – wud help lerners and asist riters jenrly.

One reason that 'cut speling' hasn't yet caught on may be due to the unintentionally comic effect of its appearance. Somehow *from ear to eternty, war and peas, hoos afrayd of verjinya wulf* and *alis in wundland* don't quite convey the effects their authors may have intended.

---

rabbi, rabbis

raccoon

raconteur

racquet *or* racket [for tennis]

radius, radii [plural]

raison detre

rancour, rancorous [rancor etc in the US]

ranunculous

rapprochement

rarefy, rarefaction

ratatouille

rateable *or* ratable

ratiocinate, ratiocination

recalcitrance, recalcitrant

reconnaissance, reconnoitre [reconnoiter in the US]

receivable

recherche

recognise *or* recognize, recognising, recognised, recognition,
  recognisance

recommend, recommendable, recommendation

recondite

recrudesce, recrudescence, recrudescent

recur, recurring, recurred, recurrence

recumbent

redundant, redundancy

refer, referring, referred, referral, reference

reggae

regime *or* régime

rehabilitate, rehabilitation

reindeer

reiterate

rejuvenate, rejuvenescence, rejuvenescent, rejuvenation

reminiscence, reminiscent, reminiscing

remuneration

renaissance *or* renascence [also the proper noun Renaissance], renascent

repellent *but* a repellant

repertoire

replace, replacing, replaced, replaceable, replacement

reprieve

repudiate, repudiation

requiescat

reredos

rescue, rescuing, rescued, rescuable

resplendent, resplendence

restaurateur

resurrection [also the proper noun Resurrection]

resuscitate, resuscitation

retrieve, retrieval, retrievable

retrousse

reveille

rhapsody, rhapsodise *or* rhapsodize

rheostat

rheumatism, rheumatoid arthritis, rheumatology

rhinoceros

rhizome

rhododendron

rhubarb

rhythm, rhythmic *or* rhythmical

ricochet, ricochetting *or* ricocheting, ricochetted *or* richocheted

riposte *or* ripost

risque

rivet, riveting, riveted

rodomontade

roommate

rotisserie

roughage

rumbustious, rumbustiously, rumbustiousness

rutabaga

Simplified Spelling Society's sensayshnl speling sistm

The Times' columnist Alan Coren greeted his readers with the news that they would be getting 10% more reading in his column because he had switched to the 'cut speling' system advocated by the Simplified Spelling Society.

"It is tru," he wrote. "This colum is but th ferst puf in th imnent tifoon: wot yu, deer reedr, ar gettin today is th same lenth as yu got last Wensdy, but it is pakt with 10 per sent more stuf, thanx to the Simplified Spelling Society."

He continued: "But the mirakl dus not stop ther: let us look at th chaptr *Furthr Advantajs* in the leflt, ware it tels how th sistm 'saves time and trubl for evryone involvd in ritn text, from scoolchildrn to publishrs, from novlists to advrtsrs, from secretaris to grafic desynrs'. We lern how they wud not only save time by ritin 10 per sent less, thus offrin freedm to persu othr displins (wot? simplifyd Rushn, cut jomtry, streemlind brane sergry?) but also benfit evrythin from producshn costs (eg smallr books etc) to th envirnmnt (eg chukin away smallr books, etc)".

But then Coren warned: " 'Incredbl!' you wil probly be shreekin at this point. 'Wot a boon this nu spelin is, sudnly th hole kulchr is lookin at brord sunny uplands. Britn will be grate agen, opn th bubly!', but ther may be, I hav to tel yu, a slite snag to al this. It bothrs me a trifl, becos I hav had a few trys at ritn difrnt tipes of stuf in th nu stile, and I think I may hav spotd wot mite be a teknikl hich wich has for sum reesn, God nose how, escaped the Sosity.

"Considr these hedlines: *'Chansler Sez No Nu Taxes: Reed Mi Lips'*; *'Man Nifes Gard in Bank Rade'*; *'Desprit Plite of Hoamles After Leeds Fludds'*. Now, can yu gess wot I am slitely wurried about? Rite, I am slitely wurried about th fact that it is abslootly impossibl to take enythin seriusly if it is ritn in th nu spelin." Little has been heard of the Simplified Spelling Society since.

---

sabbatical
saccharin [the substance]; saccharine [over-sweet]
sacrilege, sacrilegious
sacrosanct
sagacious, sagacity
samurai
sanatorium [sanitarium in the US], sanatoria *or* sanatoriums
  [plural],

sanctimonious, sanctimoniously, sanctimony

sanguine, sanguinary, sanguinely, sanguinity

sapphire

sarsaparilla

sassafras

satellite

satyr

sauerkraut

saute

savoir faire

schadenfreude *or* Schadenfreude

schematic

scherzo

schism

schizophrenia, schizophrenic, schizoid

schlemiel

schlep

schlock

schmaltz

schmuck

schnapps

schooner

schottische

sciatica

scimitar

scintilla, scintillate, scintillating, scintillation

sclerosis, sclerotic

scourge

scurrilous

scythe, scything

seance *or* seance
secateurs
secretaire
secretary, secretarial, secretariat
segue, segueing, segued
seismic, seismograph, seismoscope

Signed and Singed

The late Peter Sellers, famous for his role as Inspector Clouseau, once received a fan's request for a *'singed* photograph'. His comic genius inspired him to take one of his publicity photographs and, after burning it around the edges, sending it off to his admirer. A few weeks later the fan wrote again: "Thank you for the photograph, but could I trouble you for another as the one you sent was *signed* all around the edges".

---

seize, seizing, seized, seizure
senescent
septicaemia [septicemia in the US]
septuagenarian
sepulchre, sepulchral [sepulcher in the US]
sequestrate, sequestration
sequoia
serendipity, serendipitous
sewage [waste]; sewerage [waste system]
sexagenarian
shellac, shellacking
shenanigans

shibboleth

shillelagh

shrapnel

siege

sieve

silhouette, silhouetted

simulacrum

sinus, sinusitis

sirocco

skilful, skilfully [skillful and skillfully in the US]

skulduggery [skullduggery in the US]

slough (pron *slow* as in *cow*, a bog]; slough [pron *sluff,* to cast off]

smorgasbord

sobriquet *or* soubriquet

soi-disant

soigne *or* soignee [feminine]

soiree

soixante-neuf

soliloquy, soliloquise *or* soliloquize

somersault, somersaulting, somersaulted [*sometimes* summersault]

sommelier

somnambulism, somnambulist, somnambulation

sophomore

souffle, souffleed

soupcon

spaghetti

spalpeen

sphagnum

spina bifida

spinnaker

spontaneity

squeegee

staccato

stalactite [hanging]; stalagmite [rising]

staphylococcus

stationary [still, fixed]; stationery [writing materials]

steatopygia

stevedore

stiletto, stilettos [plural]

stoic, stoical, stoicism

storey [floor of building]; story [tale]

straight [line]; strait [sea channel]; strait-laced, strait-jacket

stratagem

strychnine

stupefy, stupefying, stupefied

styptic

suave, suavely, suavity, suaveness

subpoena, subpoenaed

subterranean

subtle, subtelty

succinct, succinctly

succour [succor in the US]

succubus

suddenness

suede

suffrage, suffragette

sulphanilamide

sumptuous, sumptuously, sumptuousness

superannuation, superannuated

supercilious

superintendent

supersede

suppository

suppress, suppressing, suppressed, suppression, suppressor

surreal, surrealism, surrealistic

surreptitious, surreptitiously

surrogate

surveillance

susceptible, susceptibility

suzerainty

sycophant, sycophantic, sycophancy

syllable, syllabic, syllabus

syllabub

sylph-like

symbiosis

symmetry

symptomatic

synagogue

synchronise *or* synchronize, synchronous, synchronicity

synonymous, synonymously

synopsis, synopses [plural]

synthesis, synthetic

syphilis, syphilitic

syringe, syringeing

syrup, syrupy

Who's teaching the teachers?

A row that erupted after a national newspaper named a school that inspectors had branded 'squalid, dangerous and riddled with truancy' ended in a scandal over the school staff's inability to spell.

After the *Sun* newspaper named East London's Hackney Free and Parochial Secondary School as being on the Education Secretary's list of failures, the deputy head and the senior teacher of the school wrote to the newspaper to complain that the inspector's critical report was three years old and that since then many improvements had been made.

Unfortunately, the letter included four glaring spelling mistakes (later claimed by the heads who wrote to be the result of haste and bad typing rather than any lack of spelling skills) – *catagory* for *category*; *substanially* for *substantially*; *overeliance* for *over-reliance* and *oudated* for *outdated*.

The Sun gleefully reproduced the letter, making sure that both 'dunce' teachers received a verbal caning from educational experts.

---

tableau, tableaux *or* tableaus [plural]

table d'hote

tagliatelli

tacit, tacitly

taciturn

tactitian

taillight

taipan

tamale

tambourine

tam-o'-shanter

tarantula

target, targeting, targeted

tassel, tasselled [tasseled in the US]

tattoo, tattooing, tattooed

tautology, tautologous, tautological

teammate

teetotal, teetotaller

telecommunications

temperance

tendentious, tendentiousness

tepee *or* teepee

tergiversate, tergiversation

teriyaki

terracotta *or* terra-cotta

terrazzo

testosterone

tete-a-tete

therapeutic

thesaurus

thief, thieves, thieving, thievery

thyme

thyroid, thyroidectomy

timpani

tinnitus

tintinnabulation

titillate, titillating, titillated, titillation

toboggan, tobogganing

toccata

tocsin [alarm bell]; toxin [poison]

tollbooth, tollgate

tomato, tomatoes [plural]

tonneau, tonneaus [plural]

tonsillitis, tonsillectomy

toque [woman's headwear]; torque [rotational force]

tornado, tornados *or* tornadoes [storm]; tournedos [beef steak]

torpedo, torpedoes

totalizator *or* totalisator

toucan

touche

toupee, toupees

Subeditors on 'supersede'

According to a survey conducted among 20 subeditors on several national newspapers, the word that causes them most problems is *supersede*. Despite checking and double checking, a printer's gremlin will somehow manage to substitute a 'c' for the 's', so to the subeditors' embarrassment the word appears as *supercede*: "On Tuesday, Mirror Group Newspapers, whose £55.05 million offer for the two papers was **superceded** by the 'dawn raid' that netted Mr O'Reilly 24.99 per cent, said it might increase its bid." (*The Times*). "Following the rise in duty in the Chancellor's late November budget, many stockists have increased their case prices. The current average case price of £68.39 **supercedes** that of £67.45 stated in the industry's 1995 review." (*Telegraph*)

---

tourniquet

trachoma, tracheostomy, tracheotomy

traffic, trafficking, trafficker

tranquil, tranquility

transatlantic

transcontinental

tranquil, tranquillise *or* tranquillize, tranquillity *or* tranquility

transcendent, transcendental, transcendentalism

transmissible

transsexual. transvestite

trauma, traumatic, traumatise *or* traumatize

triptych

triumvirate

trompe l'oeil

troop [army]; troupe [actors]

trousseau, trouseaux *or* trouseaus [plural]

tsar *or* czar, tsarina *or* czarina

tsetse fly

tuberculosis, tubercular

tunnel, tunnelling, tunnelled [tunneling, tunneled in the US]

turmeric

twelfth

tyranny, tyrannical, tyrannise *or* tyrannize

tyrannosaurus

'Ullo, 'Ullo, what's this about the police being charged with criminal spelling?

The following is a sampling of language misdemeanours committed in a London police station's crime reports. Articles reported stolen included a 'four birth tent' (for quads, presumably), a Ford Cubrololey (cabriolet), an Alpha Romeo, several garden gnombs and a carkey (khaki) jacket. Offences were committed at Hybry (Highbury) Corner and Sidnum (Sydenham), and one suspect, who gained entry to premises by forcing a 'skylark' (skylight), was described as wearing a pale blue suite. His accomplice could have been a Frenchman, as he was wearing a leather berry (beret). Fair cop, guv?

---

ubiquitous, ubiquity
ukulele *or* ukelele
ululate, ululation
umbrella
unaffected
unanimous, unanimously
unapproachable
unappropriated
unassailable
unbiassed *or* unbiased
unconscionable, unconscionably
unctuous, unctuously
unguent
unmistakeable *or* unmistakable
urethra
useable *or* usable

usury, usurer
utilitarianism

Vicissitudes of Spelling

Poor spelling is not always a serious matter. Try keeping a straight face through these student howlers, each the result of a simple spelling error:

* Russians use the acrylic alphabet
* Daniel Defoe wrote simply and sometimes crudly
* At Nelson's funeral, fifty sailors carried the beer after laying in state
* Paris was once haunted by many cortisones
* Thomas Gray wrote the *Alergy in a Country Churchyard*
* Alfred Tennyson was England's most famous poet lariat
* I enjoy reading and being embossed in a good book

vaccine, vaccination
vacillate, vacillating, vacillated, vacillation
vacuous
vacuum, vacuuming, vacuumed
variegated, variegation
vassal
vehicle, vehicular
veldt *or* veld
vendetta

ventriloquism, ventriloquist

veranda *or* verandah

verbatim

verisimilitude

vermilion *or* vermillion

verruca

veterinary, veterinarian

vicarious

vichyssoise

vicissitude

victuals, victualling, victualled, victualler

vilify, vilification

vinaigrette, vinegar

vin ordinaire

violoncello

virulence, virulent

vis-a-vis

viscose, viscosity

vituperate, vituperation

volcano, volcanoes *or* volcanos

volte-face

voluptuous, voluptuary

vouchsafe

voyeur, voyeuristic, voyeurism

vulcanise *or* vulcanize

Why Words are Shorter in America

In this list of 2,000 most misspelt words you will have noticed that where American spellings are given they are invariably shorter. Where in British English *rancour* is spelt with an *'our'* ending, in American English it is one letter shorter: *rancor*. Many thousands of *'our'* ending words are similarly simplified. Silent letters are often dropped, too, so that *catalogue* and *dialogue* in Britain become *catalog* and *dialog* across the Atlantic.

The move to simplify spellings in the US began in the early 19th century and reformers included Noah Webster, Isaac Pitman (of shorthand fame) and Mark Twain. Their urgings resulted in the establishment of the American Philological Association in 1876 but it wasn't until the industrialist millionaire Andrew Carnegie gave $250,000 to the simplified spelling cause thirty years later that things began to move. Words with alternative spellings had the longer one chopped; *judgement* became *judgment*, *axe* became *ax*, *programme* became *program*, and so on. A particular target was the unnecessary doubling of letters; why write *grovelling* when *groveling* conveyed the same meaning? (A rare exception is *wilful* in Britain but *willful* in the US). Other targets included *'oe'* and *'oeu'* words like *phoenix* and *manoeuvre* which became *phenix* and *maneuver*.

There were some misgivings, however; *tho* for *though*, *tuf* for *tough* and *yu* for *you* were among thousands of suggestions that failed to make the American dictionaries.

---

wagon *increasingly preferred* to waggon
wainscot, wainscoting *or* wainscotting
weather (climate); wether (sheep); whether (question)
werewolf

whereabouts

whereas

wherin

wherewithal

whinge

whisky (Scotch); whiskey (Irish and American)

whitlow

whole, wholly

wilful [willful in the US], wilfully, wilfulness

will-o'-the-wisp

withold, witholding

witticism

wizen, wizened

woebegone, woeful, woefully

woollen, woolly [woolen, wooly in the US]

worshipping, worshipped, worshipper [worshiping etc in the US]

wrath, wrathful

wreath [flowers]; wreathe [intertwining]

wunderkind

xerography

xylophone, xylophonist

yacht, yachting, yachtsman

yashmak

yodel, yodelling, yodeller [yodeling, yodeler in the US]

yoghurt *or* yogurt *or* yoghourt

zabaglione

zeppelin

zucchini

zwieback

The Famous Broken Rule of Spelling: I before E except after C

Of all the rules of spelling none is more capricious than the 'i' before 'e' except after 'c' rule, or, as the ancient jingle has it:

I before E
Except after C,
Or when sounded like A
As in *neighbour* or *weigh*.

As it happens, most words in the English language do follow this rule:

*   achieve, brief, fierce, relieve, shield, shriek, thief, yield
*   conceivable, deceive, perceive, receive

and those words sounding like 'ay':

*   reign, veil, beige, feint, freight, skein, rein

But what about *either*? And *heifer, weird, sovereign* and *foreign*? These are all 'ei' words in which there is no 'c'. Nor is the 'ei' in these words sounded like 'ay'.

To deal with these rule-breakers, some grammarian invented another rule: 'i' before 'e' except after 'c' and before 'g'. This effectively takes care of such words as *sovereign* and *foreign* and also of words like *height* and *sleight*, especially if you can remember this extension to the original rhyme:

I before E,
Except after C,
Or when sounded like A
As in *neighbour* or *weigh*,
Or when sounded like 'ite'
As in *height* and *sleight*.

For a while, everyone was happy. But eventually it dawned on people that still lurking in the dictionary were such outlaws as *either, seize, seizure, weird* and *heifer*. To our knowledge they are still there, still untamed by any rule or guideline except perhaps that of th renowned schoolmistress Miss Hall, who insisted that her pupils learned the following:

"Neither leisured foreign neighbour seized the weird heights during the reign of the sovereign king who forfeited the reins of government. The heir feigned that the neigh of either reindeer was due to the weight, which was eighty skeins of yarn in the sleigh."

Now, has Miss Hall apprehended all the renegades?

The Horrors of Hyphenation

The rules about when and where to use a hyphen seem to keep changing.

Only a generation or two ago everyday words such as *today* and *tomorrow* were hyphenated: *to-day* and *to-morrow*. On the other hand, many words have been unified by hyphens: *son in law* has become *son-in-law*; *hard of hearing* is now generally hyphenated as *hard-of-hearing*. And quite a few word combinations have passed through the hyphenated stage to become single words: a *book seller* became a book-seller and is now a *bookseller*; *life like* is now *lifelike* but only after spending its chrysalis stage as *life-like*.

Generally, hyphens are used to clarify the meanings of word combinations. That's why compounds such as *forgetmenot, rightofway* and *semiilliterate* are hyphenated as *forget-me-not, right-of-way* and *semi-illiterate*, while easily read combinations such as *blood pressure, olive oil* (separate word combinations), *gentleman, cupboard, newsprint* and *afterglow* (single word derivatives) are not.

The hyphen is subject to so many variations and illogical exceptions as to make rules virtually useless. Here is a handy list of words and names that are usually, but not always, hyphenated:

age-old, air-conditioning, air-cooled, air-dried, all-American, all-clear, ankle-deep, anti-abortion, armour-piercing, awe-inspiring

bandy-legged, billet-doux, black-eyed, blood-alcohol, blood-red, bloody-nosed, blue-pencil, bone-shaking, break-even, break-in, breast-fed, brick-built, bright-eyed, broad-beamed, broken-down, brother-in-law, bull's-eye, burnt-out, by-and-by

call-up, cane-backed, card-index, carpet-sweeping, catch-as-catch-can, cat-o'-nine-tails, cat's-eye, cattle-raising, check-in, city-bred, clear-cut, clean-shaven, clear-eyed, clip-clop, close-knit, closed-circuit, Coca-Cola, cold-shoulder, come-on, copper-bottomed, court-martial, co-worker, cross-channel, cross-country, cross-dressing, cross-examine, cross-purposes, crow's-foot, custom-tailored

daddy-longlegs, daughter-in-law, deaf-and-dumb, deep-freeze, deep-sea fishing, dew-laden, die-cut, dog-eared, do-it-yourself, double-barrel, double-cross, double-dealing, double-decker, double-entendre, double-park, double-quick, double-up, Dow-Jones, drip-dry, drive-in, drug-addicted, duck-billed, dust-laden

ear-splitting, earth-shaking, east-northeast etc, even-numbered, even-tempered, ever-present, ever-ready, ex-husband, ex-serviceman, extra-large

face-saving, fair-skinned, far-distant, fat-free, feeble-bodied, fever-stricken, fill-in, fine-drawn, fire-resistant, five-ply, flag-raising, flat-bottomed, flea-bitten, fleet-footed, flip-flop, fly-by-night, follow-on, foot-and-mouth disease, fore-edge, forget-me-not, four-letter word, four-o'clock (five-o'clock etc), four-part (five-part etc), free-spoken, front-end, full-grown, full-strength, fur-lined

get-together, give-and-take, go-ahead, go-between, go-getter, God-fearing, gold-plated, good-for-nothing, good-looking, grey-haired, gun-shy

habit-forming, half-and-half, half-alive, half-baked, half-breed, half-hourly, half-mast, hard-of-hearing, hard-on, half-true, half-yearly, hand-built, hand-in-hand, hand-knit, hand-me-down, hard-and-fast, hard-hat, hard-hit, hard-won, head-on, heart-throb, heart-to-heart, heaven-sent, helter-skelter, high-class, high-minded, higgledy-piggledy, high-spirited, high-tech, hit-and-miss, hit-and-run, hog-tie, hollow-eyed, home-baked, hot-blooded, how-do-you-do

ice-cold, ice-cooled, ill-advised, ill-fated, ill-treat, ill-use, in-flight, infra-red, Irish-born (British-born, American-born etc), ivy-covered

jack-of-all-trades, jack-o'-lantern, jerry-built, jet-propelled, jewel-studded, jiggery-pokery, Johnny-come-lately, jury-rigged

kiln-dry, knee-brace, knee-deep, knee-high, knock-for-knock, knock-kneed,know-all, know-how, know-it-all

lace-edged, lady-in-waiting, land-based, Land-Rover, large-scale, late-lamented, Latter-day Saint, lay-by, lean-to, left-bank, left-handed, life-size, light-headed, light-footed, light-year, like-minded, lily-white, little-known, little-used, long-awaited, long-distance, long-handled, long-legged, long-lived, loose-limbed, love-lies-bleeding, low-key, low-lying

mail-order, make-believe, man-hours, man-of-war, many-coloured, mare's-nest, mass-produced, May-day, mean-spirited, micro-organism, middle-aged, middle-of-the-road, mid-Victorian (mid-forties etc), mile-long, mother-in-law, mother-of-pearl, motor-driven, mouth-filling, mud-splashed

name-dropping, near-miss, near-sighted, needle-sharp, never-ending, never-never, ne'er-do-well, new-mown, nickel-plated, night-flying, noble-minded, non-starter,

O-level, oak-beamed, odd-job man, odd-numbered, off-season, off-licence, off-peak, off-putting, off-the-record, old-fashioned, old-maidish, on-and-off, one-night stand, one-sided, once-over, open-air, out-and-out, out-of-date, out-of-doors, out-of-the-way, over-the-counter

pace-setting, pale-faced, paper-thin, part-time, passers-by, penny-pinching, pest-ridden, photo-offset, pick-me-up, pigeon-toed, pile-driving, pitch-black, place-name, plain-spoken, pleasure-bent, pleasure-seeking, pocket-sized, point-to-point, pole-vault, post-natal, price-cutting, price-fixing, pro-Arab (pro-German, etc), public-spirited, punch-drunk, put-on

quick-change, quick-tempered, quick-witted

rat-infested, razor-keen, razor-sharp, re-cover (eg a sofa), ready-built, ready-mix, red-faced, red-hot, right-angle, right-handed, right-minded, right-of-way, ring-in, road-test, rock-climbing, roll-on roll-off, rose-scented, rough-and-ready, rough-and-tumble, rough-coat, rubber-stamped, run-in, run-on, rye-grass

St Martin-in-the-Fields, Saint-Saens, sabre-toothed, saddle-backed, sawn-off, say-so, scar-faced, second-class, second-guess, second-rate, set-aside, set-to, sharp-witted, shell-like, shilly-shally, shop-soiled, short-changed, short-circuited, short-handed, short-lived, shut-in, sign-on, silver-haired, silver-tongued, simple-minded, single-breasted, single-seater, Sino-Japanese etc, six-cylinder, six-shooter, skin-graft, sky-high, slap-up, slow-motion, small-scale, snail-paced, so-and-so, so-called, soft-boiled, soft-pedal, soft-shelled, son-in-law, spoon-fed, spot-check, spread-eagle, stage-struck, stand-in, steel-framed, stick-in-the-mud, stiff-backed, stock-still, stone-cold, stone-dead, storm-tossed, straight-backed, straight-faced, strong-arm, sub-lieutenant, sugar-coated, sun-baked, sun-dried, sure-fire, sure-footed

T-shirt, tail-ender, take-home, tax-exempt, tax-free, thought-provoking, three-cornered, three-piece, three-ply, three-ring circus, tie-break, tight-fitting, time-consuming, time-honoured, tip-off, tom-tom, tone-deaf, top-hatted, trade-in, trans-Siberian (trans-Canadian, etc but transatlantic – no hyphen), trap-door spider, trouble-free, true-blue, try-on, twenty-first (twenty-third, forty-sixth, etc), tutti-frutti, tut-tut, twice-told, two-faced, two-step, two-up

U-boat, un-American etc, uncalled-for, unheard-of, unthought-of

V-neck, velvet-pile, vice-chairman (but vice admiral, vice president etc, no hyphens)

waist-high, walk-on, walkie-talkie, washed-out, washed-up, water-cooled, water-soaked, water-soluble, wave-worn, weak-kneed, weather-beaten, weather-wise, web-footed, week-ending, week-old, weigh-in, well-being, well-bred, well-deserving, well-informed, well-known, well-read, well-spoken, well-thought-of, well-thought-out, well-to-do, well-wisher, well-worn, wet-nurse, wide-angle, wide-awake, wide-open, will-o'-the-wisp, window-cleaning, window-shopping, wire-haired, wood-panelled, work-and-turn, worm-eaten, wrong-thinking

x-ray or X-ray

+Y-chromosome, Y-fronts, year-old, year-round, yellow-bellied, young-womanhood

Z-chromosome.

The way out of hyphenation hassles is to curb your logical and investigative urges. That way you won't have to wonder why it is *mother-of-pearl* and *government-in-exile* (hyphenated) but *next of kin* and *officer in charge* (unhyphenated). And why is it *razzle-dazzle* but *razzmatazz, nitty-gritty* but *riffraff, willy-nilly* but *dilly dally, nick-knack* but *nickname*?

Don't even ask.

Problem Proper Nouns and Commonly Misspelt Names

Many of these are commonly misspelt, too – British and foreign place-names, names of people and products, medical and plant names, and proper nouns derived from names. You may not often be called upon to spell the *Mohororicic discontinuity* or the capital of Burkina Faso, *Ouagadougou*, but it could just be handy to know, in our everyday lives, that it is *Mitsubishi* and not *Mitsibushi*, that the 'butterfly bush' is a *Buddleia* and that the *Taoiseach* is the prime minister of the Irish Republic – and get the spelling right, too! Here are some of the most pernickety of these spelling challenges.

Abergavenny, Wales
Aberystwyth, Wales
Abu Dhabi, United Arab Emirates
Abyssinia
Aldeburgh, Suffolk
Appelation Controlee
Archimedes
Achilles tendon
Acquired Immunodeficiency Syndrome (Aids)

Addis Ababa, Ethiopia

Aer Lingus

Afghanistan

Afrikaans

Agamemnon

Aladdin

Albuquerque

Aldwych, London

Allegheny mountains

Algonquin Hotel, NY (but Algonquian Indians of North America)

Alsace-Lorraine

Alzheimer's disease

Amontillado sherry

Annunciation

Anorexia nervosa

Apache

Aphrodite

Apocalypse

Apollinaris mineral water

Appalachian Mountains, Appalachian

Arbroath, Scotland, Arbroath smokies

Arc de Triomphe

Aristotle, Aristotelian

Armageddon

Art nouveau

Ascension Day

Ashby-de-la-Zouch, Leics.

Ashkenazi

Athanaeum Club, London

Aubusson carpets

Auchtermuchty, Scotland

Audubon Society

Augean stables

Auld Land Syne

Auld Reekie

Aurora Borealis

Auschwitz

Axminster carpets

Azerbaijan

Babylon

Baccalaureat (more often anglicised as baccalaureate)

Bacchus, Bacchic

Baedeker (travel guidebooks)

Baghdad

Baha'i, Baha'ism

Bahrain

Balthazar

Bannockburn, Scotland

Barabbas

Bar Mitzvah

Bas Mitzvah

Bathsheba

Baudelaire

Bayeaux Tapestry

Bayreuth Festival

Bearnaise sauce

Beau Brummell

Beaufort scale

Beau Geste

Beaujolais

Beaulieu Castle, Hants

Beaune

Bechuanaland

Beelzebub

Beijing, China

Belshazzar's feast

Berchtesgaden

Betws-y-Coed, Wales

Blenheim Palace, Oxfordshire

Bletchley Park

Bloemfontein. South Africa

Boadicea (popular spelling of the more correct Boudicca)

Boccaccio

Boheme, La (opera)

Bohemia, Bohemian

Bokhara rugs

Bophuthatswana (Black South African state)

Bordeaux

Boris Godunov (opera)

Bosnia-Herzegovina

Botticelli

Boughton Monchelsea (Kent)

Bourgogne (France)

Bovey Tracey, Devon

Bovine Spongiform Encephalopathy (BSE)

Braille

Brecht, Brechtian

Britannia, Britannica (as in *Encyclopaedia Britannica*)

Brobdingnag (*Gulliver's Travels*)

Brummagem (native of Birmingham)

Buccleuch

Buchenwald

Buddha

Buddleia (popular spelling of the more botanically correct *buddleja*)

Bundestag

Byelorussia

Cadillac

Caedmon

Caernarfon (not Carnarvon), Wales

Caerphilly, Wales

Caesar, Caesarean section

Caius College, Cambridge

Camembert

Canaan

Cape Canaveral

Capodimonte porcelain

Caractacus

Caribbean

Carrara marble

Casablanca

Cerberus

Cerebral thrombosis

Cerne Abbas, Dorset

Chapel-en-le-Frith, Derbyshire

Charlemagne

Chartreuse

Chateaubriand

Chateauneuf-du-pape

Chateau d'Yquem

Cheyenne

Cincinnati

Cinque ports

Cirencester, Gloucs

Coq au vin

Coquilles St Jacques

Coliseum (London theatre)

Colosseum (Rome ampitheatre)

Comanche (N American Indian tribe)

Comedie-Francais

Comedie humaine

Compton Wyngates, Warwickshire

Concertgebouw Orchestra, Amsterdam

Connecticut

Correggio

Cosa Nostra

Cosi fan tutte (opera)

Cote d'Ivoire (former Ivory Coast)

Courtauld Institute

Creutzfeldt-Jakob disease (CJD)

Criccieth, Wales

Curacao

Cyrillic

Czechoslovakia

Christophpher is a Phphirst

Why Mrs Pia Agergaard of Copenhagen wanted to name her son Christophpher instead of simply Christopher remains a mystery, but she did — and fought a nine-year battle with with the Danish authorities to make it legal. In Denmark, parents may give children only names approved by the state and the church, and the name Christophpher was one 'ph' too far for the Court of Ecclesiastic Affairs which ruled it illegal (although they would allow Christoffer). In 1995, however, the 1982 law banning 'ridiculous' names was relaxed, Mrs Agergaard won her case and Christophpher his given name. Perhaps a pity. With such a law in Britain we wouldn't have to grapple with the spellings of Angharad, Sophronia, Deion, Iestyn, Aneurin, Sacheverell, Lakeisha, Torquil, Meironwen and Zedekiah, all gaining in popularity.

Dadaism. Dadaist
Daguerrotype
Dail Eireann (Republic of Ireland parliament)
Daiquiri (Cuban rum, thence the cocktail)
Dalai Lama
Daphnis and Chloe
Dardanelles
Darjeeling
Debrett (short for *Debrett's Peerage*, the aristocrats bible)
Deity, the
Dejeuner sur l'herbe (Manet's famous painting)
Demoiselles d'Avignon (Picasso's famous painting)

Demosthenes

Des Moines

Deuteronomy

Deutschmark

Dien Bien Phu

Dionysus

Disraeli, Benjamin

Djibouti (East African republic)

Dobermann pinscher

Dolgellau, Wales

Domesday Book

Don Juan

Don Quixote

Doppelganger

D'Oyly Carte Opera Company

Dungeness, Kent

Dun Laoghaire, Ireland

Dunsinane (Shakespeare's *Macbeth*)

Ebbw Vale, Wales

Ecclesiastes

Ecumenical Council

Edgbaston, Birmingham cricket ground

Edinburgh

Eichmann Trial

Eiffel Tower

Eisteddfod

Elysee Palace, France

Emmentaler cheese

Encyclopaedia Britannica

Endymion, the lover of Selene in Greek mythology; Keats's poem;
   Disraeli's novel

Entre-Deux-Mers

Epaminondas

Epernay

Epiphany

Epithalamion (Spenser's poem)

Erewhon (Samuel Butler's novel)

Eroica Symphony

Euripides

Eurydice (and Orpheus)

Eustachian tube

Excalibur

Existentialism

Ezekiel

Exocet (missile)

Faberge (jewelled eggs)

Faerie Queene, The (Spenser's great poetic work)

Faeroes (North Atlantic island group)

Fair Isle (knitwear)

Fauves, Les

Feock, Cornwall

Fernet Branca

Filipino

Finistere, France

Fledermaus, Die (Strauss opera)

Folies-Bergere

Fontainebleau

Forsyte Saga

Fraulein, Frau

Fuhrer, Der

Fujiyama (or Mt Fuji, *not* Mt Fujiyama)

Fu Manchu, Dr (Chinese movie detective)

Fyffes (banana exporting company)

Grass Roots of Spelling

Names of plants, flowers and trees are a real trap for anyone who writes about gardening. Here are some of the tricky ones:

Agapanthus, Amaranthus, Amaryllis, Anemone, Antirrhinum, Aquilegia, Aspidistra, Aubrieta, Bignonia, Bougainvillea, Buddleia, Calycanthus, Camellia, Ceonothus, Chrysanthemum, Convolvulus, Cotoneaster, Cyananthus, Cymbidium, Cytisus, Dahlia, Deutzia, Dryopteris, Eucalyptus, Freesia, Fuchsia, Gypsophila, Hyacinth, Impatiens, Liquidambar, Narcissus, Nymphaea, Pelargonium, Philodendron, Phlox, Pieris, Pyracantha, Rhododendron, Strelitzia, Stephanotis, Tradescantia, Weigela, Yucca

---

Galapagos Islands

Gallipoli

Gandhi, Mohandas Karamchand

Gauguin, Paul

Geffrye Museum, London

Genghis Khan

Gethsemane

Gewurztraminer

Gioconda, La (Mona Lisa)

Givenchy

Glyndebourne Festival

Gnostic

Gobelins Tapestry

Godalming, Surrey

Goethe

Gomorrah

Gondoliers, The (Gilbert and Sullivan opera)

Gonzalez, Byass sherry

Goonhilly Downs

Gorgonzola

Gotterdammerung

Graf Zeppelin

Grand Guignol

Gruyere cheese

Guadeloupe, Caribbean

Guangdong (formerly Kwangtung)

Guatemala

Guggenheim Museum, New York

Guinevere

Guinness

Gujarati, the people and language of the Indian state Gujarat

Gulbenkian Foundation

Gurkha

Gypsy or gipsy

UNLIKELY PLACE NAMES

Helions Bumpstead and other unlikely English place-names

Britain abounds in bizarre place-names, from familiar rib-ticklers such as Nether Wallop, Upper Slaughter, Upton Snodsbury, Little Snoring, Much Wenlock, High Sticker, Thannnington Without, Barton in the Beans and Mousehole to rather lesser-known signposts: Ugley, Sewer's End, Upper Dicker, Sixpenny Handley, Mucking, Up Exe, Bottoms, Wig Wig, Splatt and Clatter. In fact it would be difficult to tell whether many village names are real or invented: there's a fine line between Mappowder-in-Plush (Dorset) and Chillwell-Before-Serving (invented).

But amusement can give way to frustration when spelling difficulty is added to such unlikely conjunctions: Ocle Pychard, Okeford Fitzpaine, Kirkley Foggo, Lytchett Maltraves, Kingston Pagpuize, Wendy-cum-Shingay, Stockleigh Pomeroy and Perranzabuloe are just a few examples. A long way from the small town in Michigan called, simply, 'Y'.

Haarlem, Holland; but Harlem, New York.

Habakkuk

Habeas Corpus

Hallelujah Chorus

Hallowe'en

Hannukah, Jewish festival sometimes called and spelt Chanukkah

Hare Krishna

Hawaii, Hawaiian

Heraklion, Crete

Herodias

Herstmonceux, Sussex

Hippocratic Oath

Hiroshima

Ho Chi Minh

Hogmanay

Holofernes

Holyroodhouse, Scotland

Houdini

Houyhnhnms (talking horses in *Gulliver's Travels*)

Huguenot

Words that always end in 'ise'

Many people are confused by words that end with the suffixes *'ise'* and *'ize'*. In hundreds of cases the use of either is optional (usually *'ize'* in the US and increasingly so in Britain) as with oxidise/oxidize, sanitise/sanitize, tyrannise/tyrannize.

But for some words there is no such option; they are *always* spelt with an *'ise'* ending. It's well worth parking these in the back of your memory to avoid future confusion:

advertise	demise	excise	premise
advise	despise	exercise	reprise
apprise	devise	exorcise	revise
arise	disenfranchise	franchise	rise
chastise	disguise	improvise	supervise
circumcise	enfranchise	incise	surmise
comprise	enterprise	merchandise	surprise
compromise		mortise	televise

But watch out for *prise* (to force open) and *prize* (reward, or to value).

Iago
Ightham, Kent
Ile de la Cite, Paris
Illinois
Immelmann turn (aerobatics)
Indianapolis
Innisfail, Ireland
Internationale, the (Socialist hymn)
Inuit (North American Eskimos)
Inveraray Castle
Iolanthe (Gilbert and Sullivan opera)
Iroquois
Ishmael
Istanbul

Jacuzzi
Jaipur, India
Jakarta, also often spelt Djakarta
Jehoshaphat
Jekyll and Hyde
Jeroboam
Jervaulx Abbey, North Yorkshire
Jodrell Bank
Judaism
Juilliard School of Music, New York
Juneau, Alaska
Jungian psychology

Kafka, Franz, **Kafkaesque**
Kalahari Desert
Kalashnikov
Kama Sutra

Katmandu, Nepal

Kazakhstan

Kewpie doll

Keynesian, Keynesianism

Khartoum

Khmer Rouge

Kircudbright, Scotland

Kirkintilloch, Scotland

Kirriemuir, Scotland

Kiwanis

Knaresborough

Koskiusko, Mt (Australia)

Krakatoa volcano

Kubla Khan (Coleridge's poem); Kublai Khan (Mogul emperor)

Kuomintang

Kyrie eleison

Llanfair PG . . . and the rest

Britain's ultimate hard-as-hell-to-spell place-name champion is undoubtedly the village in Anglesea, Wales – Llanfair PG. But that is only the tenth of it, for its full name is

LLANFAIRPWLLGWYNGYLLGOGERYCHWYRNDROBWLL-LLANTYSILIOGOGOGOCH

the literal translation of which is 'The Church of Saint Mary in the hollow of white hazel near to the rapid whirlpool and to Saint Tysilio's Church near to a red cave". With its 58 letters the name also appears to be a world-beater; the runner up being a New Zealand place called *Taumatawhakatangihangakoauauotamateapokai-whenuakitanataua* (57 letters).

La donna e mobile (aria from Rigoletto)

Laertes

La Guardia Airport, New York

Lalique glass

Languedoc, France

Laphroaig, Scotch whisky

Lascaux Caves, France

Lausanne, Switzerland

Legionnaire's disease; sometimes Legionnaires' disease

Leicestershire

Leighton Buzzard, Bedfordshire

Leipzig, Germany

Liebfraumilch

Liechtenstein

Liege

Lilliput, Lilliputian

Lindbergh (famous solo pilot whose baby was kidnapped)

Lindisfarne, Holy Island off Northumberland coast

Linguaphone

Linlithgow, Scotland

Linnaeus, Linnaean, Linnaean Society

Lipizzaner (Austrian performing horses)

Ljubljana, Slovenia

Llandaff, Wales

Llandrindod Wells, Wales

Llandudno, Wales

Llanelli, Wales

Llangollen, Wales

Llareggub (the 'spelt backwards' town in Dylan Thomas's *Under Milk Wood*)

Loathe (verb, to hate)

Loth (adjective, reluctant)

Lohengrin

Looe, Cornwall

Louis Quinze

Lourdes, France

Louvre, Paris

Lucia di Lammermoor (Donizetti's opera)

Lufthansa

Luxembourg

Lyonnaise

Lysistrata (Aristophanes' comedy)

Lost Beauties of English Spelling

In 1874 the lexicographer Charles Mackay published *Lost Beauties of the English Language*, in which he bemoaned the fact that several thousand words in the language had fallen from use. For bad spellers this was good news, but on the other hand many of the lost words were colourfully expressive, as these few examples show:

alderliefest	dearest	*benothinged*	defeated
embranglement	perplexing	*groundstalworth*	firm
jobbernowle	thickhead	*losengerie*	lying
mawwallop	badly cooked	*tapsalterie*	topsy-turvy
spousalbreach	adultery	*wanchancie*	unlucky

Maastrich, Holland

Mabinogion (Ancient Welsh tales)

Maccabees

McCarthyism

Machiavelli, Machiavellian

Machu Picchu, Peru

Maeterlinck, Maurice

Mackintoshes Toffee

Macintosh (waterproof coat)

Madame Tussaud's

Maecenas

Magdelen College, Oxford

Magdalene College, Cambridge

Mahabharata (Sanscrit epic poem)

Mahdi (Muslim messiah)

Mahe, Seychelles

Mah-Jongg

Maigret, Inspector

Majolica (opaque glazed pottery)

Malacca

Malagasy (former Republic of Madagascar)

Malawi (formerly Nyasaland)

Malmesbury, Wiltshire

Malthus, Thomas; Malthusian, Malthusianism

Mancunian

Manon Lescaut (Abbe Prevost's novel and Puccini's opera)

Manzanilla dry sherry

Mao Tse-tung, or Mao Zedong

Mappa Mundi

Maraschino cherries

Mardi Gras

Margaux, Chateau

Marrakech, or Marrakesh, Morocco

Marseillaise, the

Marseille, France

Marylebone, London

Massachusetts

Mato Grosso

Mau Mau (former Kenyan nationalist movement)

Maupassant, Guy de

Meccano

Mediterranean

Mehitabel

Meissen porcelain

Menai Strait

Mennonite religion

Mephistopheles

Mesopotamia

Messerschmitt

Methuselah

Meursault white wine

Michaelmas

Michelangelo

Middlesborough

Milwaukee, Wisconsin, USA

Minneapolis, Minnesota, USA

Minnehaha

Minotaur

Miserables, Les (Victor Hugo's novel)

Mississippi

Missolonghi, Greece

Missouri

Mistinguette (Paris music hall star)

Mitsubishi

Mnemosyne (goddess of memory)

Mobius loop

Mobutu Sese Seko, deposed Zairean president

Moby-Dick, *not* Moby Dick

Mogadishu, Somalia

Mohammed

Mohave Desert

Mohican Indians

Moholy-Nagy, Laszlo (Hungarian-US photographer)

Mohorovicic discontinuity

Moliere

Monegasque (citizen of Monaco)

Montaigne, French essayist

Montessori teaching system

Montezuma, Montezuma's revenge

Montmarte, Paris

Montparnasse, Paris

Montreaux Festival

Mont-Saint-Michel, France

Montserrat, West Indies (but Nicholas Monsarrat, author of *The Cruel Sea*)

Morocco

Morte D'Arthur (Malory's Arthurian legends); Morte d'Arthur (Tennyson's poem)

Moulin Rouge, Paris

Munchhausen, Baron; Munchhausen's syndrome

Mussorgsky, Modest Petrovich (Russian composer)

Mustapha Kemal (Turkish leader)

Mycenae, Mycenaean civilisation

My Lai massacre

Narcissus

Nassau, Bermuda

Navaho Indian tribe

Navratilova, Martina (tennis star)

Neanderthal Man

Nebuchadnezzar

Nefertiti

Nehru, Jawaharlal

Nestle

Neuilly, Paris

Nietzsche, Friedrich; Nietzschean

Nihilism, Nihilist

Nijinski, Vaslav (dancer and choreographer)

Nkrumah, Kwame, former president of Ghana

Nostradamus

Novaya Zemlya, Arctic island group

Nuits-Saint-Georges, France

Nuneham Courtenay, Oxfordshire

Nurburgring grand prix motor racing circuit, Germany

Nyerere, Julius (first president of Tanzania)

Obadiah

Oberammergau, Bavaria

Odysseus

Odyssey, the (Homer's epic poem)

Oedipus, Oedipus complex

Oerlikon gun

Oistrakh, David (Russian violinist)

Olympian, Olympiad

Omar Khayyam

Omdurman, Battle of

Oradour massacre, France

Orpheus and Eurydice

Orrefors glass

Oswestry, Shropshire

Oundle, Northamptonshire

Ouagadougou, capital of Bukina Faso

Ouija board

Ozymandias (Shelley's sonnet)

Problem Plurals

Good spelling includes the correct spelling of plurals, which often trips people up. One group of words is especially troublesome: compound terms such as *mother-in-law, inspector general, court martial* and *passer-by*. The plurals of these are, respectively, *mothers-in-law, inspectors general, courts martial* and *passers-by*. You will note that when forming plurals of such compound terms, it is the significant word that becomes plural: *mother, inspector, court* and *passer*. In these cases the first word is the significant one, and is therefore the one pluralised. But in other cases it is the last word that becomes the plural: *assistant attorney* (*assistant attorneys*); *trade union* (*trade unions*); *vice chancellor* (*vice chancellors*) and *major general* (*major generals*). There are also compounds in which the significant word is in the middle: *assistant* **chiefs** *of staff, deputy* **comptrollers** *general*, etc. And, just to add some extra pain, there are compounds in which <u>no</u> word is significant: *will-o'-the-wisps, pick-me-ups, forget-me-nots*. Finally, when a noun is hyphenated with an adverb or preposition, the noun becomes the plural (*listeners-in, goings-on, lookers-on*) and when neither word in the compound is a noun, the last word is pluralised: *also-rans, go-betweens, higher-ups, tie-ins, etc.*

Paganini, Niccolo (Italian violinist and composer)

Palatinate

Paleolithic Age

Paleozoic Era

Palladian architecture

Panmunjom, Korea

Papeete, Tahiti

Paraclete

Paraguay, Paraguayan

Paraquat

Parisienne

Passchendaele (Belgian World War I battlefield)

Pathetique, the (Beethoven piano sonata)

Pavarotti, Luciano

Pavlovian

Peloponnesian War

Penmaenmawr, Wales

Pennsylvania

Pentateuch

Pepys's Diary

Petulengro (popular Gypsy name)

Pevsner, Nikolaus (art historian)

Phaedra (Greek mythology); Phaedrus (Roman writer); Phaethon (Greek Mythology)

Pharaoh

Pharisee

Pheidippides (Greek athlete)

Philadelphia

Philippines

Piccadilly, Piccadilly Circus, London

Piedmont

Pierrot

Pinocchio

Piraeus, Greece

Pitlochry, Scotland

Pittsburgh, USA

Plaid Cymru (Welsh nationalist party)

Pleiades (star cluster)

Pleistocene

Pocahontas

Poiteres, France

Pollyanna

Pompeii

Pompidou Centre, Paris

Pont-L'Eveque cheese

Pontypridd, Wales

Popocatepetl (Mexican volcano)

Portuguese

Poseidon

Poughkeepsie, New York

Pre-Raphaelite, Pre-Raphaelitism
Presbyterian
Prestatyn, Wales
Prix Goncourt
Psalter
Ptolemy, Ptolemaic
Punt e Mes (Italian apertif)
Puvis de Chavannes (French painter)
Pygmalion
Pyongyang, North Korea
Pyramus and Thisbe
Pyrrhic victory
Pythagoras, Pythagoras's Theorem

Qaddafi, Muammar el-, often Gadhafi (ruler of Libya)
Qantas
Qatar
Quai d'Orsay, Paris
Quasimodo
Quattrocento
Quebecois
Quirinale, Rome
Quonset hut
Qwa Qwa (South African black homeland)

Rachmaninov, Sergei
Rabelais, Rabelaisian
Ramadan
Ranunculus
Rashomon (classic 1951 Japanese movie)
Rastafarian

Rauschenberg, Robert (US pop painter)

Rechabites (friendly society)

Reichstag, Berlin

Rembrandt, Rembrandtesque

Renaissance

Reykjavik, Iceland

Rhesus (Rh) factor

Richelieu, Cardinal

Richthofen, 'Red Baron' (World War I German flying ace)

Riefenstahl, Leni (German filmmaker)

Rievaulx Abbey, Yorkshire (qv Jervaulx Abbey)

Rijksmuseum, Amsterdam

Riyadh, Saudi Arabia

Robespierre (French revolutionary leader)

Rockefeller Center, New York

Roget's Thesaurus

Rolleiflex

Rolls-Royce (*not* Rolls Royce)

Romania, Romanian, sometimes Roumania, Roumanian

Rontgen, Wilhelm

Roosevelt, Franklin Delano

Roquefort cheese and dressing

Rorschach test

Rosencrantz and Guildenstern

Rosenkavalier, Der (Strauss opera)

Rosh Hashanah (Jewish New Year)

Rosicrucian

Rotherhithe, London

Rothschild

Rousseau, Jean-Jacques (philosopher); Henri (painter)

Roussillon

Rubaiyat of Omar Khayyam

Rumpelstiltskin

Runnymede, Surrey

Ruysdael, Jacob (Dutch painter)

Rwanda

Ryukyu Islands, Japan

SaccoVanzetti trial

Sacre-Coeur, Paris

Sagittarius

Saint-Saens

St-Germain, Paris

Salmonella

Salzburg Festival

Samson Agonistes (Milton's poem)

Santayana, George (philosopher)

Sarajevo, Bosnia-Herzegovina

Sartor Resartus (Carlyle's satire)

Saskatchewan, Canada

Sassenach

Savile Club, London

Saxe-Coburg-Gotha

Saxmundham, Suffolk

Scheherazade

Schiaparelli, Elsa (couturier)

Schleswig-Holstein

Schoenberg, Arnold (composer)

Schopenhauer

Schumann, Robert (composer)

Schwarzenegger, Arnold

Schwarzkopf, Elizabeth (German soprano); 'Stormin' Norman' (US Army general)

Schweppes

Scorcese, Martin (film director)

Scylla and Charybdis

Sennacherib

Sequoia

Sevastopol, Unkraine

Sevres porcelain

Shakespearean or Shakespearian

Shangri-La

Shenandoah

Shepheard's Hotel, Cairo

Shi'ite or Shiah (Muslim sect)

Shoeburyness, Essex

Siegfried

Sierra Leone

Sikh

Sinai, Mt

Sinn Fein

Sioux Indian tribe

Sisyphus, Sisyphean

Skopje, Macedonia

Slivovitz (plum brandy)

Sodom and Gomorrah

Sohrab and Rustum (Matthew Arnold's epic)

Solihull, near Birmingham

Solzhenitsyn, Alexander (Russian novelist)

Sophocles, Sophoclean

Sorbonne, Paris

Spandau (Berlin jail where Nazis were held); Spandau Ballet (pop
  group)

Stanislavsky, Konstantin (acting teacher)

Stockhausen, Karlheinze (German composer)

Stoke Poges, Buckinghamshire

Stornoway, Outer Hebrides

Stradivarius

Struwwelpeter (children's storybook character)

Sturm und Drang

Subbuteo

Sudetenland

Sumer is icumen in (13th century English poem)

Svengali

Swahili

Sylphides, Les (ballet)

Syracuse, Sicily; also New York

Taj Mahal

Tammany Hall

Tanganyika

Tannhauser (Wagner opera)

Taoisach (Irish prime minister)

Tauchnitz editions

Tchaikovsky, Pyotr Il'yich (Russian composer)

Tecumseh (Shawnee Indian chief)

Teesside

Tegucigalpa, Honduras

Tehran, Iran

Telemachus

Tennessee

Terpsichore, Terpsichorean

Thermopylae, Greece

Thessaloniki, Greece; sometimes Salonika

Thyssens (German industrialist family)

Tiananmen Square, Beijing

Tierra del Fuego

Tiffany

Timbuktu, Mali; also Tombouctou and, popularly, Timbuctoo

Timotei shampoo

Tipperary, Ireland

Titicaca, Lake

Tocqueville, Alexis (French political scientist)

Tokugawa (Japanese shoguns)

Tolpuddle Martyrs

Tonton Macoute (Haiti death squads)

Torquemada, Tomas (Spanish Inquisitor)

Toulouse-Lautrec, Henri

Tourette's syndrome

Toynbee Hall, London

Trawsfynydd, Wales

Triboro' Bridge, New York

Troilus and Cressida

Trossachs, Scotland

Trovatore, Il (Verdi opera)

Tschiffeley's Ride

Tuareg

Tutankhamen

Tynwald (Isle of Man parliament)

Tyrolean

Uccello, Paolo, Italian painter
Ulaanbaatar, Mongolia; more popularly, Ulan Bator
Ulysses
Unter den Linden, Berlin
Uriah Heep (Dickens' character)
Uruguay, Uruguayan
Uttar Pradesh, India
Uttoxeter
Uzbekistan

Valkyries
Valenciennes, France
Valhalla
Valletta, Malta
Valparaiso, Chile
Van Heusen shirts
Vanuatu, formerly New Hebrides
Vargas Llosa, Mario (Peruvian novelist)
Velasquez, Diego (Spanish painter)
Venezuela
Versailles
Veuve Clicquot champagne
Vientiane, Laos
Vietcong, Vietminh
Vieux Carre, New Orleans
Vinho verde
Vladivostok, Russian Siberia
Vlaminck, Maurice (French painter)
Vonnegut, Kurt (American novelist)
Vouvray
Vuillard, Edouard (French painter)

'ware Welsh!

In the Principality of Wales there is still a substantial amount of Welsh spoken, and even more written. Names that English-speakers know and love – Brecon Beacons, Snowdonia, Cardiff and Holyhead, for example, can, on a signpost or a map, change to *Bannau Brycheiniog, Eryri, Caerdydd* and *Caergybi* respectively. The Welsh are always sympathetic to the vain efforts of outsiders trying to master their language, and you will earn respect by being able to spell correctly at least a few of the names important to their history and culture. Try these:

Cymru	Wales
Dewi Sant	St David, patron saint of Wales
Rhodri Fawr	The king who united Wales
Llewelyn	A Welsh king who died in 1240
Dafydd ap Gwilym	Famous 14th century Welsh poet
Owain Glyn-dwr	Created the first Welsh parliament

Waikiki Beach, Hawaii

Walpurgis Night

Watteau, Jean-Antoine (French painter)

Wedgwood pottery

Wehrmacht

Weimaraner (dog breed)

Welwyn Garden City, Hertfordshire

Wensleydale

Wickhambreaux, Kent

Wiener schnitzel

Wilhelmstrausse, Berlin

Windhoek, Namibia

Winnie-the-Pooh

Witwatersrand, South Africa

Wolfenden Report

Wollstonecraft, Mary (British feminist)

Woolf, Virginia

Wooloomooloo, Sydney

Wootten Bassett, Wiltshire

Worcestershire, Worcestershire sauce
Wroxeter, Shrewsbury
Wykehamist
Wynken, Blynken and Nod

Xanadu (fabled city of Coleridge's poem, *Kubla Khan*)
Xanthippe (Socrates' shrill wife)
Xerxes
Xhosa

Yangtze Kiang, or Yangtze River, China
Yaounde, Cameroon
Yom Kippur
Yosemite National Park, USA
Ypres, Belgium
Yves Saint Laurent

Zaire
Zeebrugge, Belgium
Zeitgeist
Ziegfeld Girls
Zeppelin
Zimbabwe
Zimmer frame
Zinoviev letter
Zoroaster, Zoroastrianism
Zouave
Zuider Zee, Holland

Kingsley Amis on Spelling

The late novelist Sir Kingsley Amis had firm views on correct grammar and spelling (expressed in *The King's English*).

On spelling, he had two arguments for avoiding incorrect spelling. One was that "the neglect of this precaution goes down badly with people, including some who may be thought generally unworthy but whose disapproval may be worth avoiding".

The second argument, he wrote, was more in the nature of an appeal. "If writing is worth doing it should be done as well as possible. Waiting at table is also worth doing, and simple pride should prevent a waiter from serving from dirty plates and with dirty hands." And so it goes with spelling.

A Novel Spelling Test

Hemingway Jones was a brilliant tale-teller, but no publisher had yet accepted any of his work. The trouble was, Hemingway couldn't spell. He intended to buy a computer (which would of course have a spellchecker) with the money from his first advance, but meanwhile . . . if only he had someone to correct his spelling, he'd be a famous novelist in no time! So why not help him? Here are the opening paragraphs of his new novel, *The Biege Bhudda of Baghdad*. You be his ever-alert editor and spot his mistakes.

The Biege Bhudda of Baghdad

The old vetrinarian paused under the verandah, perspiring in his kakhi jacket. It was at least ninety farenheit. Mosquitos wirred over his head and, crouching under the fuchsias an iguano flicked it's evil tongue at him, iridescent in the flourescent glow of the parrafin lamp.

It had been a long day. First, he'd vacillated Mrs Horner's chihwahwa for diptheria and pneumonia.

The poor animal had sqirmed and writhed so much that the needle had perpetrated Mrs Horner's prosterior instead; now he could look forward with certainety to a lawsuite. Then there was that hysterical hippopotomus with a predeliction for *homeo sapiens*. And, finally, the marahraja's parrakeet with the swollen proboscis and a fine vocabluary of words not suitable for the ears of young ladies decided to expire.

The old vet sank wearily down on the chaise longue near the rhododendhrons, poured himself a generous shot of Irish whisky, and considered his dilemna. Would he continue here and risk a coronory, or take up the more congenial post at the armadillo park in the Carribean?

Novel Spelling Test: Corrections

If Hemingway Jones had used the following spellings, his novel might stand a better chance of being published:

Biege *is incorrect for* Beige		Bhudda *is incorrect for* Buddha	
Bagdhad	Baghdad	vetrinarian	veterinarian
verandah	veranda	kakhi	kahki
farenheit	fahrenheit	wirred	whirred
iguano	iguana	flourescent	fluorescent
parrafin	paraffin	it's	its
vacillated	vaccinated	chihwahwa	chihuahua
diptheria	diphtheria	sqirmed	squirmed
perpetrated	penetrated	prosterior	posterior
certainety	certainty	lawsuite	lawsuit
hippopotomus	hippopotamus	predeliction	predilection
homeo sapiens	*homo sapiens*	marahraja's	maharajah's
parrakete	parakeet	vocabluary	vocabulary
rhododendhrons	rhododendrons	dilemna	dilemma
coronory	coronary	Carribean	Caribbean

Phew! And all those errors were in Hemingway Jones's first few paragraphs!

So how good a subeditor were you? If you spotted 20 spelling mistakes that's a reasonable score; anything from 25 to 30 is excellent. And if you know the correct spelling of each wrongly spelt word, that's remarkable! There is no such thing as Irish whisky, by the way; whisky is exclusive to Scotland and Scotch. It should be Irish *whiskey*. And a pat on the back if you corrected *it's* to *its*.

Collins Wordpower Terminal Test of Spelling Skill

The 'Terminal Test' (or 'Super Test', 'Killer Bee', Death By Spelling' – call it what you will) is a battery of twenty exercises in detecting faulty spelling. Each exercise concerns a different facet of life and knowledge, from brand names to birds, from dogs to drinks, from composers to countries of the world.

Each exercise consists of 20 words or names, some of which are correctly spelt, and some of which are not. Your task is to identify the misspelt words – those you *know* are misspelt and those you *think* are misspelt. Allowing one point for each word, the total score for getting everything absolutely right is 20x20 or 400 points.

Score as you go; the answers are in the next section (pp 159-166). Deduct two points each time you miss spotting a misspelt word in each test. Also deduct two points for any word you think is misspelt but is not. Thus, in Test No.1, if you failed to identify two misspelt words, and also thought a correctly spelt word was misspelt, you have to deduct 3 x 2 = 6 points, resulting in a score of 14 for that test. Not exactly brilliant, but not a disaster, either.

How to rate your spelling ability

When you have checked and scored each of the 20 tests that follow, and totalled your scores, how do you stand in the spelling stakes? Here's a guide:

Any score from 380-400	Superspeller of the Year!
350-378	Superspeller, Gold Medal
320-348	Superspeller, Silver Medal
300-318	Above average, very good
250-298	Slightly below average, but nothing to be ashamed about
Below 250	Keep working at it!

Alternatively, your ego might benefit from a handicapped test, as explained on page 160. Discard your five lowest lowest scores for the 20 spelling tests, and compare your points score for the 15 remaining tests against the handicap total of 300. Any score over 250 points would still count as a considerable spelling achievement, and a score of 200 or more would be above average.

Countries of the World

The names of a number of the nations listed below are misspelt. Can you identify them? For each mistake you miss deduct 2 points; for each correctly spelt country you thought was misspelt, also deduct 2 points. Deduct these points from the total of 20; that is your score for this test.

1   Burkina Faso

2   Quatar

3   Liechtenstein

4   Tuvalu

5   Afganhistan

6   Eritrea

7   Djibouti

8   Zimbabwee

9   Tristan da Cunha

10 Mauritania

11 Montserrat

12 Uruguay

13 Andora

14 Peurto Rico

15 Turks and Caicos Islands

16 Sri Lanka

17 Bhutan

18 Ruwanda

19 Kazakhstan

20 Guyuana

Score: **/20**

COUNTRIES OF THE WORLD

Brand Names

Some of these band names are misspelt. Can you spot them? For each mistake you miss deduct 2 points; for each correctly spelt name you thought was misspelt, also deduct 2 points. Find your score by deducting these from the total of 20

1   Sweet 'n Low

2   Albran

3   Brylcream

4   Weight Watchers

5   Gillette

6   Baddedas

7   Moet and Chandon

8   Budweiser

9   Jaccuzzi

10   Mr Wippy

11   Levi's

12   Schaparelli

13   Lamborghini

14   Guinness

15   Butioni

16   Caddilac

17   Colman mustard

18   Austen Reed

19   Aquascutum

20   Lea and Perrins

Score: **/20**

BRAND NAMES

Film and Entertainment

Some of these names are misspelt. Can you identify which ones? For each mistake you miss deduct 2 points; for each correctly spelt name you thought was misspelt, also deduct 2 points. Deduct these points from the total of 20 for your score.

1   Shirley MacLaine
2   Roman Polanski
3   Gina Lollabrigida
4   Frederick March
5   Warren Beatty
6   Joseph Cotton
7   Michelle Pfeiffer
8   Winona Rider
9   Marcello Mastroanni
10 Stephanie Beacham
11 Simone Signoret
12 Jon Voight
13 Richard Prior
14 Cybil Shepherd
15 Bela Lugosi
16 Catherine Deneuve
17 Bridget Bardot
18 Ben Kingsley
19 Arnold Swartzenegger
20 Kris Kristofferson

Score: /20

Illnesses and Medicines

See if you can detect which of these medical terms are misspelt. For each spelling error you miss, deduct 2 points; also deduct 2 points for each correctly spelt term you thought was misspelt. Deduct these points from the total of 20 for your score.

1 bulimina
2 dyspepsia
3 prostate gland
4 tintinitis
5 chromosone
6 gastroenteritis
7 barbiturate
8 apolexy
9 sclerosis
10 leukaemia
11 delirium tremens
12 conjunctivitis
13 erogonous zone
14 glaucoma
15 psychosomatic
16 hemorhoids
17 medecine
18 resuscitation
19 mumps
20 eczema

Score: **/20**

Mythology

Can you spot the misspelt mythological names below?
Deduct 2 points for each misspelt name you miss, and also deduct
2 points for every correctly spelt name you thought was misspelt.
Deduct these points from the total of 20 for your score.

1 Dionysius

2 Argonauts

3 Hesperides

4 Juventus

5 Lacoon

6 Odysseus

7 Heracles

8 Agamemnon

9 Aphrodite

10 Posiedon

11 Adriadne

12 Achilles

13 Zeus

14 Cerebrus

15 Sagitarius

16 Icarus

17 Illiad

18 Minotaur

19 Eurydice

20 Oeudipus

Score: /20

MYTHOLOGY

Art and Artists

Do you know which names below are misspelt? For each misspelt name you miss deduct 2 points, and for each correctly spelt name you judged was misspelt also deduct 2 points. Deduct these from the total of 20 points for your score.

1   Giacometti

2   Andy Warohl

3   Vincent van Gogh

4   Boticelli

5   Velasquez

6   Pissarro

7   Bruegel

8   Tintoretto

9   Bracque

10   Milais

11   Caravaggio

12   Pre-raphaelite

13   L S Lowery

14   Watteau

15   Rembrant

16   Sir Edward Burne-Jones

17   Toulouse-Lautrec

18   Maguritte

19   Le Corbusier

20   Jackson Pollock

Score: **/20**

Writers and Writing

If you can spot every misspelt name here you score a full 20 points, but if not, deduct 2 points for each misspelt name you miss, and two points for each correctly spelt name you thought was misspelt. Deduct these points from the total of 20 for your score.

1   Anita Bookner
2   Salman Rushdie
3   P G Woodehouse
4   Brendan Behan
5   V S Naipaul
6   Alexandr Solzhenitsyn
7   Gore Vidale
8   John Betjamin
9   Max Beerbohm
10 Jean-Paul Sartre
11 Vladimir Nabakov
12 Lawrence Durrel
13 A E Houseman
14 William Shakespeare
15 J P Dunleavy
16 Simone de Beauvoir
17 J R R Tolkien
18 Virginia Wolfe
19 Agatha Christie
20 Brian Aldiss

Score: **/20**

The Bible

Some of these names are misspelt. Can you identify which ones? For each mistake you miss deduct 2 points; for each correctly spelt name you thought was misspelt, also deduct 2 points. Deduct these points from the total of 20 for your score.

1   Jeremiah
2   Hittites
3   Barrabas
4   Gallilee
5   Pharisees
6   Gesthemene
7   Sennacherib
8   Passover
9   Ninevah
10 Heroditas
11 Ephiphany
12 Ananias
13 Pentateuch
14 Basheba
15 Armaggedon
16 Samson
17 Elijah
18 Pharoah
19 Gommorah
20 Nickodemus

Score: /20

The Winged World

Do you know which of these bird names are misspelt? For each misspelt name you miss spotting, deduct 2 points, and also 2 points for every correctly spelt name you thought was misspelt. Deduct these points from the total of 20 for your score.

1   chaffinch
2   hoopoe
3   kookuburra
4   curlew
5   tarmigan
6   windchat
7   shrike
8   bustard
9   kittywake
10 dunnoch
11 fieldfare
12 albatros
13 pippit
14 chough
15 goosehawk
16 lyre bird
17 greebe
18 ring ouzel
19 guillemot
20 toucan

Score: /20

The World of Dogs

Can you spot the misspelt doggie names below? Lose 2 points for each misspelt name you miss, and also lose 2 points for every correctly spelt name you thought was misspelt. Deduct your lost points from the total of 20 for your score.

1 Sealyham terrier
2 Afghan hound
3 Weimariner
4 basenji
5 shih-tzu
6 Rotweiller
7 Pekinese
8 keeshond
9 borzoi
10 saluki
11 Pomeranian
12 daschund
13 Airdale
14 pappilion
15 lhasa apso
16 Doberman Pinchser
17 basset hound
18 schnauzer
19 schipperke
20 Dandie Dinmont

Score: /20

Food and Eating

If you can spot every misspelt name here you score a full 20 points, but if not, deduct 2 points for each misspelt name you miss, and two points for each correctly spelt name you thought was misspelt. Deduct these points from the total of 20 for your score.

1 proscuttio
2 mozzarella
3 salade nicoise
4 licquorice
5 ratatouille
6 brioche
7 broccoli
8 petit poir
9 Worcstershire sauce
10 Caerphilly cheese
11 persimmon
12 mulligatawny soup
13 Dolcelata cheese
14 vinigrette
15 picalilly
16 yoghurt
17 paella
18 tamarsalata
19 blancmange
20 Camembrert

Score: /20

Drinks and Drinking

Some of these drinks are mish – sorry – misspelt. Can you identify which ones? For each misspelling you miss deduct 2 points, and also for each correctly spelt drink you thought was misspelt. Deduct these points from the total of 20 for your score.

1 Drambuie
2 Calvardos
3 semmilon
4 Heineken
5 Agnostura bitters
6 Dubonnet
7 Valpollicella
8 Beaujolais
9 Ouzo
10 Verdichio
11 sauterne
12 daiquiri
13 Sambucca
14 Chartreuse
15 Grolsch
16 mint julip
17 tecquila
18 margerita
19 Mickey Finn
20 Pouilly-Fuisse

Score: **/20**

Foreign Words and Phrases

Can you spot the misspelt words and phrases? Lose 2 points for each misspelt word or phrase you miss, and also lose 2 points for each correctly spelt word or phrase you thought was misspelt. Deduct your lost points from the total of 20 for your score.

1   ad nauseam
2   pot-pourri
3   vive la difference
4   zietgiest
5   nobless oblige
6   carte-de-visit
7   que sera sera
8   churchez la femme
9   in vino veritas
10 sotto voce
11 frito misto
12 habeus corpus
13 abseil
14 tempis fugit
15 mea culpa
16 pari-mutuel
17 non compis mentis
18 hoi polloi
19 pret-a-porta
20 san froid

Score: **/20**

British Place-names

Do you know which of these place-names are misspelt? For each misspelt name you miss spotting, deduct 2 points; and also 2 points for every correctly spelt place-name you thought was misspelt. Deduct these points from the total of 20 for your score.

1   Aberystwyth, Cardigan
2   Inverarey Castle, Argyle
3   Wroxeter, Shropshire
4   Picadilly Circus, London
5   Glynebourne, Sussex
6   Chapel-en-le-Frith, Derby
7   Oswestry, Cheshire
8   Cirencester, Gloucestershire
9   Beaulieu Castle, Hampshire
10 Hamstead, London
11 Lyme Regius, Dorset
12 Slough, Berkshire
13 Wednesbury, Staffordshire
14 Plaidstow, Sussex
15 Todmorton, Yorkshire
16 Yeovil, Somerset
17 Widness, Lancashire
18 Utoxetter, Staffordshire
19 Oundle, Northamptonshire
20 Bury St Edmunds, Suffolk

Score: **/20**

Music and Musicians

Can you spot the misspelt music-related names below? Lose 2 points for each misspelt name you miss, and also lose 2 points for each correctly spelt name you *thought* was misspelt. Deduct your lost points from the total of 20 for your score.

1   violincello
2   glockenspiel
3   Mendlesohn
4   Paganini
5   Hindmithe
6   Deutsche Grammophon
7   sinfonetta
8   Monserat Caballe
9   Mussorgsky
10 arpeggio
11 Rachmaninov
12 tocatta
13 Barbarolli
14 Prokofiev
15 saxophone
16 Yehudi Menhuin
17 Pachelbel
18 Saint-Saens
19 pianofort
20 Palestrina

Score: /20

The Scientific World

Can you spot the misspelt words and names? Lose 2 points for each misspelt word or name you miss, and also lose 2 points for each correctly spelt word or name you believed was misspelt. Deduct your lost points from the total of 20 for your score.

1   polymer
2   flocculant
3   Joddrell Bank
4   haemogoblin
5   Archimedes
6   brontusaurus
7   bhutane
8   diesel
9   enzyme
10 saccarin
11 Gallileo
12 Joseph Priestley
13 incandescence
14 kilowat
15 Andromeda constellation
16 aluminium
17 polyesther
18 coefficient
19 pterodactyl
20 testosterone

Score: /20

153

History

Do you know which of these historical names and places are misspelt? For each one you miss spotting, deduct 2 points; and also lose 2 points for every correctly spelt name you thought was misspelt. Deduct these points from 20 for your score.

1   Marie Antoinette
2   Ghandi
3   Nuremburg
4   Thermopylae
5   Gorbachov
6   Ho Chi Minh
7   Knossos
8   Versailles
9   Dr Crippin
10   Kahrtoum
11   Mussolini
12   General Eisenhower
13   Tutankhamun
14   Anne Boleyn
15   Nelson Mandala
16   Mata Hari
17   Biafara
18   Dag Hammarskjold
19   Golda Mier
20   General De Gaulle

Score: **/20**

The Sporting Life

Can you spot the misspelt sporting names below? Lose 2 points for each misspelt name you miss, and also lose 2 points for each correctly spelt name you believed was misspelt. Deduct these lost points from the total of 20 for your score.

1   Emil Zapotek
2   Sterling Moss
3   Tour de France
4   Joe DiMaggio
5   potholing
6   Billy Jean King
7   Lindford Christie
8   Minnesota Fats
9   Michael Schumacher
10 Richie Benaud
11 Par Lhap
12 Pat Eddery
13 Jayne Torvill
14 tobogganing
15 Ivan Lendel
16 Nicky Lauda
17 Muhamhad Ali
18 Jack Nicklaus
19 Severiano Ballesteros
20 Steffi Graff

Score: /20

Antiques

Spot *all* the misspelt names and terms and score 20 points. But lose 2 points for each misspelt word you miss and also 2 points for each correctly spelt word or name you thought was misspelt. Deduct the lost points from 20 for your score.

1   Faberge
2   Sothebys
3   candalabra
4   jardiniere
5   Sevres
6   chifonnier
7   Stradavarius
8   armoire
9   cloisonne
10 turreen
11 Palladian
12 alabaster
13 Wedgewood
14 mahogany
15 ottomann
16 Hepplewaite
17 netsuke
18 chandelier
19 Quatrocentro
20 escritoire

Score: **/20**

Potpourri

For the 20th and final spelling quiz in the *Collins Wordpower Terminal Test* you are asked to read the following sentences, quite a few of which contain a spelling mistake. The same scoring rules apply: for every error you miss you lose 2 points, and for every correctly spelt word you believed was misspelt you also lose 2 points. Deduct any lost points from the total of 20 for your score.

1 Most people know that Samuel Taylor Coleridge wrote the poem *The Rhyme of the Ancient Mariner*.

2 Silicone Valley in California is now regarded as the hub of the world's computer industry.

3 The Dreyfus affair remains one of the most disturbing episodes in modern French social and political history.

4 A week before the Chancellor's budget the word leaked out that the health and welfare services faced swingeing cuts.

5 The pioneering work on genes won both scientists Noble laureates.

6 F Scott Fitzgerald's *The Great Gadsby* is easily one of America's ten best novels of the 20th century.

7 The fussiness of Brussels' lawmakers is in deep contrast to the laissez-faire attitudes of European nations a century ago.

8 Most people know at least a few of the songs of Rogers and Hammerstein.

9 More and more people who have witnessed a painful death are coming around to the benefits

of euthanasia.

10 The defending champion's occasional inability to duck fast enough is considered by many to be his Achilles' heel.

11 These days, medical science has virtually eliminated diseases such as tuberculosis, hooping cough and smallpox.

12 The dramatis personae of the extravaganza included almost all the cast of the long-running television series *The Adams Family*.

13 What do you say to a Southern Swiss: *auf Wiedersehen* or *arrividerci*?

14 Nobody would dispute that the late newspaper tycoon Robert Maxwell was a thorough-going melagomaniac.

15 Bill Gates is supposed to be as rich as Croesus.

16 Few people can quickly convert a temperature expressed in Celsius to one expressed in Fahrenheit.

17 The committee studied the latest audit of the countrys' renewable resources.

18 What ever happed to Pavlova's dog and Planck's constant?

19 One of the strangest phenomena of World War II was the seemingly endless supply of Japanese pilots for kamikaze duty.

20 The mystery surrounding Marylin Monroe's death feeds a publishing industry with at least a dozen books every year.

Score: /20

Answers

to Collins Wordpower Terminal Test of Spelling Skill

Read these notes before checking the answers and marking your scores

In this Machiavellian marathon of spelling skill, several things can happen. During the road-testing of the 20 quizzes, many spelling hopefuls were disappointed that they lost just as many points by wrongly identifying correctly spelt words as misspelt as they did by not spotting the real culprits. But knowing when a word is spelt correctly is just as important a skill as recognising and correcting a misspelling.

While the twenty categories of subject matter are judged to cover what most people might be expected to know at least something about as part of their general knowledge, the depth of this knowledge from category to category is bound to be somewehat uneven. A person *au fait* with the worlds of entertainment and sport is very likely to outspell another who hardly ever watches television or goes to the movies. A well-read person might romp through the *Writers and Writing, Mythology* and *History* categories, but struggle with *Brand Names* and totally unable to tell whether it's a Heineken or a Hieneken.

It could be assumed that aside from those people with a vast depth of general knowledge this unevenness should balance out between one person and another. So don't be too discouraged if, with some of the categories with which you are not on familiar terms, you achieve embarrassingly low scores – other contenders for the spelling crown will have similar disappointments.

So what should one do to avoid too many bruised egos? What approach would, say, the great Dr Johnson take? As a dictionary maker (and no mean speller!) the great man would understandably expect every citizen to spell well. But as a humanitarian he would undoubtedly have sympathy with those of us – the great majority – who could never hope to approach his mastery of a language that since his day is growing in size and complexity at an unprecedented rate.

Our guess is that he would suggest throwing away the results of your five lowest-scoring tests. So instead of matching your score over 20 tests against the ultimate total of 400 points, you would match your fifteen best scores against a handicap total of 300. Of course, if you have scored brilliantly (say 350 points or more against the total of 400) you'll ignore Dr Johnson's suggestion.

Now, are you ready? Here are the answers.

Countries of the World

There are 7 misspellings: Qatar, not Quatar; Afghanistan, not Afganhistan; Zimbabwe, not Zimbabwee; Andorra, not Andora; Puerto Rico, not Peurto Rico; Rwanda, not Ruwanda; and Guyana, not Guyuana.

Brand Names

Ten misspelt brand names: All Bran, not Albran; Brylcreem, not Brylcream; Badedas, not Baddedas; Moet et Chandon, not Moet and Chandon; Jacuzzi, not Jaccuzzi; Mr Whippy, not Mr Wippy; Schiaparelli, not Schaparelli; Buitoni, not Butioni; Cadillac, not Caddilac; Austin Reed, not Austen Reed.

Film and Entertainment

Nine misspelt names: Gina Lollobrigida, not Lollabrigida; Fredric March, not Frederick; Joseph Cotten, not Cotton; Winona Ryder, not Rider; Marcello Mastroianni, not Mastroanni; Richard Pryor, not Prior; Cybill Shepherd, not Cybil; Brigitte Bardot, not Bridget; Arnold Swarzenegger, not Swartzenegger.

Illnesses and Medicines

There are 7 spelling mistakes: bulimia, not bulimina; tinnitus, not tintinitis; chromosome, not chromosone; apoplexy, not apolexy; erogenous zone, not erogonous; hemorrhoids, not hemorhoids; medicine, not medecine.

Mythology

There are nine misspelt mythological names: Dionysus, not Dionysius; Juventas, not Juventus; Laocoon, not Lacoon; Poseidon, not Posiedon; Ariadne, not Adriadne; Cerebus, not Cerebrus; Sagittarius, not Sagitarius; Iliad, not Illiad; Oedipus, not Oeudipus.

Art and Artists

There are eight misspelt names: Andy Warhol, not Warohl; Botticelli, not Boticelli; Braque, not Bracque; Millais, not Milais; Pre-Raphaelite, not Pre-raphaelite; L S Lowry, not Lowery; Rembrandt, not Rembrant; Magritte, not Maguritte.

Writers and Writing

Eight writer's names were misspelt: Anita Brookner, not Bookner; P G Wodehouse, not Woodehouse; John Betjeman, not Betjamin; Vladimir Nabokov, not Nabakov; Lawrence Durrell, not Durrel; A E Housman, not Houseman; J P Donleavy, not Dunleavy; Virginia Woolf, not Wolfe.

The Bible

Nine Biblical names were misspelt: Barabbas, not Barrabas; Galilee, not Gallilee; Gethsemane, not Gesthemene; Herodias, not Heroditas (*the wife of King Herod who urged her daughter Salome to ask for John the Baptist's head on a plate*); Epiphany, not Ephiphany; Bathsheba, not Basheba; Armageddon, not Armaggedon; Pharaoh, not Pharoah; Nicodemus, not Nickodemus.

The Winged World

If you're one of Britain's millions of bird-lovers you'll have scored well in this test. There were 9 misspelt names: kookaburra, not kookuburra; ptarmigan, not tarmigan; winchat, not windchat; kittiwake, not kittywake; dunnock, not dunnoch; albatross, not albatros; pipit, not pippit; goshawk, not goosehawk; grebe, not greebe

The World of Dogs

You will have noticed the seemingly haphazard way in which the names of some dog breeds are capitalised, while others are not. The explanation for this is just as bewildering, so you will not be penalised if you have mistakenly corrected a non-capitalised breed to a capitalised one, and vice versa.

There were 7 misspelt breeds: Weimaraner, not Weimariner; Rottweiler, not Rotweiller; Pekingese, not Pekinese; dachshund, not daschund; Airedale, not Airdale; papillon, not pappilion, Doberman Pinscher, not Pinchser.

Food and Eating

There were nine misspellings: prosciutto, not proscuttio; liquorice, not licquorice; petits pois, not petit pois; Worcestershire sauce, not Worcstershire; Dolcelatte cheese, not Dolcelata; vinaigrette, not vinigrette; piccalilly or piccalilli, not picalilly; taramasalata, not tamarsalata; Camembert, not Camembrert.

Drinks and Drinking

Ten misspellings: Calvados, not Calvardos; semillon, not semmilon; Angostura bitters, not Agnostura; Valpolicella, not Valpollicella; Verdicchio, not Verdichio; sauternes, not sauterne; Sambuca, not Sambucca; mint julep, not julip; tequila, not tecquila; margarita, not margerita.

Foreign Words and Phrases

There were ten misspelt words or phrases. You will not be penalised for committing crimes against diacritical marks. The mistakes are: Zeitgiest, not zietgiest (must be capitalised); noblesse oblige, not nobless; carte-de-visite, not carte-de-visit; cherchez la femme, not churchez; fritto misto, not frito; habeas corpus, not habeus; tempus fugit, not tempis; non compos mentis, not compis; pret-a-porter, not porta; sang froid, not san froid.

British Place-names

How aware are you of your surroundings – the place called the British Isles? There were 9 misspelt place-names: Inveraray Castle, not Inverarey; Piccadilly Circus, not Picadilly; Glyndebourne, not Glynebourne; Hampstead, not Hamstead; Lyme Regis, not Regius; Plaistow, not Plaidstow; Todmorden, not Todmorton; Widnes, not Widness; Uttoxeter, not Utoxetter.

Music and Musicians

Did you spot the nine spelling errors? They were: violoncello, not violincello; Mendelssohn, not Mendlesohn; Hindemith, not Hindmithe; sinfonietta, not sinfonetta; Monserrat Caballe, not Monserat; toccata, not tocatta; Barbirolli, not Barbarolli; Yehudi Menuhin, not Menhuin; pianoforte, not pianofort.

The Scientific World

There were eight misspellings: Jodrell Bank, not Joddrell; haemoglobin, not haemogoblin; brontosaurus, not brontusaurus; butane, not bhutane; saccharin, not saccarin; Galileo, not Gallileo; kilowatt, not kilowat; polyester, not polyesther.

History

There were nine misspelt names: Gandhi, not Ghandi; Nuremberg, not Nuremburg; Gorbachev, not Gorbachov; Dr Crippen, not Crippin; Khartoum, not Kahrtoum; Tutankhamen, not Tutankhamun; Nelson Mandela, not Mandala; Biafra, not Biafara; Golda Meir, not Mier.

The Sporting Life

Nine misspellings: Emil Zatopek, not Zapotek; Stirling Moss, not Sterling; Billie Jean King, not Billy; Linford Christie, not Lindford; Phar Lap, not Par Lhap; Ivan Lendl, not Lendel; Niki Lauda, not Nicky; Muhammad Ali, not Muhamhad; Steffi Graf, not Graff.

Antiques

There were nine misspelt names and terms from the antiques business: Sotheby's, not Sothebys (the possessive apostrophe signifies Sotheby's Auctions, and also applies to Christie's and other auction houses); candelabra, not candalabra; chiffonier, not chifonnier; Stradivarius, not Stradavarius; tureen, not turreen; Wedgwood, not Wedgewood; ottoman, not ottomann; Hepplewhite, not Hepplewaite; Quattrocento, not Quatrocentro.

Potpourri

There were eleven 'disguised' spelling errors in this test and if you managed to identify nine or ten you can consider yourself an extremely adroit speller indeed! Here they are:

1   The poem that Coleridge actually wrote was *The <u>Rime</u> of the Ancient Mariner*, not *Rhyme*.

2   The Californian computer hotbed is <u>Silicon</u> Valley, not Silicone Valley (which could be nearby, in Hollywood . . .).

5   Noble they may be, but the scientists would have won <u>Nobel</u> laureates.

6   Fitzgerald's novel was entitled *The Great Ga<u>t</u>sby*.

8   But *Ro<u>d</u>gers and Hammerstein* wrote better tunes.

11 The disease is *whooping cough*, not hooping cough.

12 The show was called *The Addams Family*, not
    Adams.

14 The late tycoon was a *megalomaniac*, not a
    melagomaniac.

17 Did you spot the misplaced apostrophe? *Country's*,
    not countrys'. If the committee had been studying
    the audit of several countries it would have been
    "countries' renewable resources".

18 Pavlova's dog never existed, but *Pavlov's dog* did.

20 The great Hollywood sex symbol was *Marilyn
    Monroe*, not Marylin.

Appendix A:

Ways to improve your spelling

This book offers a number of ways to help you improve your spelling. These are listed here, along with a few other ideas you might like to try.

1. Learn the basic rules of spelling; See Appendix B

2. Use mnemonics, which are jingles or patterns which jog your memory, to help you remember words which you find difficult to spell. You will find them in many entries in this book. If you don't know or can't find one which exists for a particular word you want to remember, try making up your own. Examples of mnemonics are:

   there's **a rat** in sep**arat**e
   it is ne**cess**ary to have one **c**ollar (**c**) and two **s**ocks (**s**)

3. Break the word down into smaller parts, and learn each small part separately. This is recommended for a number of words in this book.

4. Visualize a difficult word. Try to remember its letters and the shape they make. This will give you a feel for whether a word looks right or wrong when you write it down.

5. Exaggerate the pronunciation of the word in your head. Sound out all the letters, including any silent letters.

6. Look at the word, cover it up, attempt to write it down, then check to see if you are correct. Keep doing this until you spell the word correctly.

7. Write out the word many times in your own handwriting, until you feel it flows without you hesitating.

8. If you spell a word wrongly, make a note of the error. You can learn to recognize the mistakes you tend to make and so prevent yourself from repeating them.

9. Make a habit of looking up any word which you are not absolutely sure about in a good dictionary.

Appendix B:

Some spelling rules:

Here are some basic spelling rules. If you recognize and remember these rules, it will help you to spell a difficult or unfamiliar word.

1. **a.** A final silent E is dropped when an ending which begins with a vowel is added, for example:
   abbreviate+ion > abbreviat+ion = abbreviation
   argue+able > argu+able = arguable
   fascinate+ing > fascinat+ing = fascinating

   b. This E is retained for the endings -CE or -GE when these letters keep a *soft* sound, for example:
   change+able = changeable
   courage+ous = courageous
   outrage+ous = outrageous

2. When the *adverb suffix* -LY is added to an *adjective* which ends in a consonant followed by -LE, the -LE is usually dropped. For example:

gentle+ly > gent+ly = gently
idle+ly > id+ly = idly
subtle+ly > subt+ly = subtly

3.   When an ending which begins with a vowel is added to a word which ends in a single vowel plus a consonant, the consonant is doubled if the *stress* is on the end of the word or if the word has only one part. For example:

admit+ance > admitt+ance =admittance
begin+ing > beginn+ing = beginning
equip+ed > equipp+ed = equipped

4.   When an ending which begins with a vowel is added to a word which ends in a single vowel plus L, the L is doubled. For example:

    cancel+ation > cancell+ation = cancellation
    excel+ent > excell+ent = excellent
    fulfil+ing > fulfill+ing = fulfilling

5.   When an ending which begins with E, I, or Y is added to a word which ends in C, a K is also added to the C to keep its *hard* sound. For example:

panic+ing > panick+ing = panicking

An exception is *arc, arced, arcing*.

6.   When the *adjective suffix* -OUS or -ARY is added to a word which ends in -OUR, the U of the -OUR is dropped. For example:

glamour+ous > glamor+ous = glamorous

honour+ary > honor+ary = honorary

humour+ous > humor+ous = humorous

7. When an ending is added to a word which ends in a consonant plus **y**, the **y** changes to **i** (unless the ending added already begins with **i**). For example:

beauty+ful > beauti+ful = beautiful

carry+age > carri+age = carriage

woolly+er > woolli+er = woollier

8. a. The *plural* of a word which ends in a consonant plus **y** is made by changing the **y** to **i** and adding **-es**, for example:

accessory > accessori+es = accessories

diary > diari+es = diaries

whisky > whiski+es = whiskies

b. The *plural* of a word which ends in a vowel plus **y** is made by adding **s**, for example:

jersey+s = jerseys

journey+s = journeys

whiskey+s = whiskeys

c. The *plural* of a word which ends in **s**, **x**, **z**, **sh**, or **ch** is made by adding **-es**, for example:

bus+es = buses

focus+es = focuses

d. The *plural* of a word which ends in -EAU is made by adding **s** or **x**, for example:

bureau+s = bureaus or

bureau+x = bureaux

gateau+s = gateaus or

gateau+x = gateaux

9. When AL- is added as a *prefix* at the beginning of a word to make a new word, it is spelt with one L. For example:

al+ready = already

al+though = although

al+together = altogether

10. The *suffix* -FUL is always spelt with one L, for example:

faithful

grateful

hopeful

11. The "uss" sound at the end of an *adjective* is almost always spelt -OUS, for example:

courageous

courteous

luscious

12. I before E except after C, when they make the sound "ee". For example:

fierce

niece

relieve

but *ceiling*
deceive
receive

13. **a.** The name or names of areas on the map begin with a capital letter:
Britain
Mediterranean

    b. The name of a religious group or its teachings begins with a capital letter:
Buddhism

Appendix C:

The Apostrophe

These are the places where the apostrophe should be used:

1. In shortened forms of words or combinations of words, the apostrophe appears in the place where a letter or letters have been missed out:

do+not > do+nt = don't
it+is > it+s = it's
they+are > they+re = they're

2. **a.** An apostrophe with the letter **s** is added to a *noun* to indicate that something else which is mentioned belongs to or relates to it:

James's cat
last week's news

b. An apostrophe alone is added to a *noun* that is already a *plural* <u>with</u> an **s**:

the winners' medals
in three weeks' time

c. An apostrophe with the letter **s** is added to a *noun* that is already a *plural* <u>without</u> an **s**:
    children's books
    men's clothes

d. **It's** does not indicate "something that belongs to it". That is **its**, without an apostrophe. **It's** is the shortened form of **it is**.

e. The *pronouns* that already indicate that something is owned by or relates to them have no apostrophe:
    hers
    ours
    theirs
    yours

3. An apostrophe is not used to form a *plural* unless it is for a letter, number, or some other short word which rarely has another plural form:
    Mind your p's and q's
    A row of 1's and a column of 2's

Appendix D:

American Spellings

The main differences in U.S. spellings from the British spellings are

1. British words which end in **-OUR** are usually spelt **-OR** in the U.S.:

   favor

   glamor

   rumor

2. British words which end in **-RE** are usually spelt **-ER** in the U.S.:

   center

   liter

   theater

3. a. British words which end in **-IZE** or **-ISE** are always spelt **-IZE** in the U.S.:

   apologize

   emphasize

   recognize

b. Those which end in -YSE are spelt -YZE:

analyze

breathalyze

4. Some words containing AE or OE in Britain always have E on its own in the U.S.:

anesthetic

diarrhea

maneuver

5. A final L is <u>not</u> doubled when an ending which begins with a vowel is added:

canceled

jeweler

Collins Wordpower

English is the most widely used language in the world, yet it is also one of the easiest languages to be misunderstood in. The Collins Wordpower series is the ultimate in user-friendliness for all who have wished for an authoritative, comprehensive yet accessible range of guides through the maze of English usage. Designed for ease of use and illustrated by top cartoonists, these books will enrich your powers of communication – whether in speech, writing, comprehension or general knowledge – and they are fun to use!

PUNCTUATION
0 00 472373 2
How to handle the 'nuts and bolts' of English prose £5.99

GOOD GRAMMAR
0 00 472374 0
How to break down the barriers between you and clear communication £5.99

SUPER SPELLER
0 00 472371 6
How to master the most difficult-to-spell words and names in the English language £5.99

GOOD WRITING
0 00 472381 3
How to write clear and grammatically correct English £5.99

VOCABULARY EXPANDER
0 00 472382 1
How to dramatically increase your word power £5.99

ABBREVIATIONS
0 00 472389 9
The complete guide to abbreviations and acronyms £5.99

FOREIGN PHRASES
0 00 472388 0
The most commonly used foreign words in the English language £5.99

WORD CHECK
0 00 472378 3
How to deal with difficult and confusable words £5.99